T0300751

NEURODIVERSE RELATIONSHIPS

Autistic and Neurotypical Partners Share Their Experiences

JOANNA PIKE

with

DR TONY ATTWOOD

Foreword by Dr Tony Attwood

Jessica Kingsley *Publishers*
London and Philadelphia

www.different-together.co.uk provides support and information for
neurotypicals (NTs) living with a partner with Asperger's Syndrome (AS)

First published in 2019
by Jessica Kingsley Publishers
73 Collier Street
London N1 9BE, UK
and
400 Market Street, Suite 400
Philadelphia, PA 19106, USA

www.jkp.com

Copyright © Different Together 2019
Foreword copyright © Tony Attwood 2019

Library of Congress Cataloging in Publication Data
A CIP catalog record for this book is available from the Library of Congress

British Library Cataloguing in Publication Data
A CIP catalogue record for this book is available from the British Library

ISBN 978 1 78775 028 9
eISBN 978 1 78775 029 6

Printed and bound in the United States

'One of the most informative, realistic and useful books I have read on the topic of AS/non-AS relationships. This book is totally unique and unlike any other I have read. It offers the reader an insight into both perspectives of an AS/non-AS relationship as both partners share honestly and openly how they experience each other.

In addition, Professor Tony Attwood offers his valuable experience, expertise and knowledge explaining and answering questions at the end of each couple's section. It is guaranteed that any reader in a similar situation will find themselves identifying with the couples in this superb book. I highly recommend this book for couples, individuals and professionals who work in this area.

Well done Joanna for putting this book together and thank you for making me smile with your humorous sketches!'

– *Maxine Aston, author of* The Other Half of Asperger Syndrome, Aspergers in Love *and* The Asperger Couples Workbook

'This is a revolutionary book: it looks at each issue from the point of view of both AS and NT partners, and both gain even more with Tony Attwood's comments. It is really helpful.'

– *Susanna Todd, Director of Different Together, NT spouse*

'A treasure trove of experiences, perspectives and strategies to enlighten and inspire every professional's practice, *Neurodiverse Relationships* is a unique collection of relationship stories and a glimpse into the diversity of AS/NT relationships with invaluable insights on the most significant challenges neurodiverse couples are navigating together.'

– *Natalie Roberts, The Asperger's Relationship Coach*

'Finally a perspective on neurodiverse relationship dynamics for yourselves, family and friends! This book gives experiential descriptions showing the impact of the array of inherent differences.

I found Tony Attwood's comments at the end of each chapter immensely helpful because they put into context each partner's experience in a meaningful way.

Highly recommended!'

– *Clare Hargrave, early childhood education specialist, NT spouse of related interest*

The Autism Spectrum Guide to Sexuality and Relationships
Understand Yourself and Make Choices That Are Right for You
Dr Emma Goodall
Forewords by Dr Wenn Lawson and Jeanette Purkis
ISBN 978 1 84905 705 9
eISBN 978 1 78450 226 3

When Herscue Met Jomphrey and Other
Tales from an Aspie Marriage
Herscue Bergenstreiml
ISBN 978 1 84905 696 0
eISBN 978 1 78450 211 9

Marriage and Lasting Relationship with Asperger's
Syndrome (Autism Spectrum Disorder)
Successful Strategies for Couples or Counselors
Eva A. Mendes
ISBN 978 1 84905 999 2
eISBN 978 0 85700 981 4

Asperger Syndrome (Autism Spectrum Disorder)
and Long-Term Relationships
Fully Revised and Updated with DSM-5® Criteria (2nd edition)
Ashley Stanford
ISBN 978 1 84905 773 8
eISBN 978 1 78450 036 8

The Other Half of Asperger Syndrome (Autism Spectrum Disorder)
A Guide to Living in an Intimate Relationship with a Partner
Who Is on the Autism Spectrum (2nd edition)
Maxine Aston
ISBN 978 1 84905 498 0
eISBN 978 0 85700 920 3

Contents

Foreword

DR TONY ATTWOOD

This book will provide a unique insight into the minds of couples where one partner has a diagnosis of Asperger's syndrome. It is the first of its kind to provide perspectives from both sides on given topics in an attempt to help couples in neurodiverse relationships understand one another better. If you are in a relationship where one of you has Asperger's syndrome, this book will help change your relationship and your life for the better.

There are common themes that arise when a couple, or one of the couple, in an AS/NT relationship seeks counselling. This book covers twelve of the most frequently experienced problems, with each couple telling it how it is (from the AS perspective) and how it feels (from the NT perspective).

When you fall in love with an Aspie, the initial stages of the relationship can feel extraordinarily intense, and the attention lavished upon you hard to resist. Commonly, however, it is not long before there is a realization that the relationship is not what was originally anticipated. The initial intense feelings of love, compassion, tolerance and understanding are slowly eroded by experience. The NT partner identifies characteristics of the AS partner that have become irritating or depressing. Emotions, experiences and responsibilities are not shared; needs and expectations are not fulfilled; communication breakdowns occur; conflicts arise over priorities and increased anxiety can lead to control issues. The NT partner can experience a change in his or her own sense of identity as previously enjoyed experiences, such as social occasions, become less and less frequent, and feelings of isolation and loneliness within the relationship increase.

Often, the NT partner gradually and reluctantly starts to 'mirror' the Aspie partner's behaviour, lifestyle and thinking in order to maintain the relationship. The AS partner may also feel irritated and depressed, feeling unable to meet his or her partner's expectations in terms of social experiences, expression of inner thoughts and feelings, intimacy, coping with change and household responsibilities – from budgeting to taking care of children. Stress for the AS partner can be considerable due to not understanding criticism for contributing to a disappointing relationship and why his or her natural behaviour should cause such distress and anguish. The AS partner may not intuitively know what to do to rectify the relationship and may feel guilt, shame and a sense of failure.

While all couples experience some of the above challenges and can make adjustments to maintain the relationship, when one of the partners has the characteristics of AS, the degree of those challenges and adjustments is far greater and the strategies to repair or improve the relationship can seem elusive to both partners. Different Together has created *Neurodiverse Relationships* as an aid for both partners to better understand one another's needs, expectations and perspectives.

This book has been written with each couple taking on a particular problem area within their relationship. We hope it will be of help to readers navigating what it means to be 'different together'.

Glossary of Terms

AS Asperger's syndrome

ASC Autism Spectrum Condition

Aspie a term used to describe a person living with Asperger's syndrome, commonly used by those with AS to describe themselves

Aspergerese communicating in a way that people with AS will more easily understand

Love languages five distinct ways of showing and receiving love that will resonate at different levels for different people. These are: words of affirmation, acts of service, receiving gifts, quality time and physical touch

Neurodiverse relationship a relationship in which one partner is neurotypical and another is on the autistic spectrum or shows neurologically atypical behaviour

Neurotypical (NT) not displaying autistic or other neurologically atypical patterns of thought or behaviour

Traffic light system a system of using colours to identify feelings or emotions, such as red for angry, green for calm, etc. This same system can also be used with numbers or words that carry particular meanings

Acknowledgements

This book has been a long time coming to fruition and an even longer time since my first thoughts of it four years ago. It is the book that I would love to have been able to read at the start of my own AS/NT-aware journey. I am convinced it would have helped my husband and me to understand one another better and to learn how to really communicate in ways that worked for both of us. With a better understanding of AS and of one another's needs and a strong motivation from us both to improve our relationship, life would have been a lot less frustrating!

Thanks must first go to all the couples who have given so much of themselves – their time, energy and honesty into sharing what life is like from their own perspectives within an AS/NT relationship. It will not have been an easy task.

I will always be grateful to Tony Attwood, who has been an inspiration to me and without whom this book would not have been written. Tony has provided an essential part of the concept of this book – that of a professional 'take' on each partner's perspective and answers to questions on each topic.

Nor could this book have been written without the dedication and commitment of one particularly inspiring woman, Lucy Carman. Lucy has spent endless hours in between husband, children and work, collating, editing, proofreading and encouraging to make this book a reality. Thank you, thank you, thank you!

Introduction

Have you ever felt as though your life resembled that of the main character in the film *Groundhog Day*? Are patterns of behaviour that lead to disagreements between you consistently being repeated despite your determination that things will change and be better next time? Have you or your partner breathed a huge sigh of relief when handed a diagnosis of Asperger's syndrome, believing that things can only get better – only to find they don't? Me too.

My partner's diagnosis of Asperger's syndrome was simply that – a diagnosis. We left the office for the four-hour drive home without any further advice. There was no recommended reading, suggested support groups, a 'what to do now' sheet or list of helpful organizations to contact. We talked on the way home about the different ways each of us had experienced relief at the diagnosis. For my partner it was, he said, finally understanding why he'd felt as he had throughout his childhood, school and relationships, 'as though living behind frosted glass'. His diagnosis gave me validation that I was not 'completely mad' or 'the only one with a problem', as he'd often accused me of being. But, beyond each other and the diagnosis, there was no ongoing support.

We hope this book will provide some helpful insights and support to those AS/NT couples struggling to understand one another's perspective.

For many of the couples who contributed to this book anonymity was a necessary part of their commitment to participate.

Ironically, the reason for anonymity is also, in part, what drove the need to write the book. There is still a stigma attached to the word 'autistic'. For those so-called 'high-functioning' autistic individuals (those with Asperger's syndrome) who often succeed in jobs ranging from law, finance, IT and engineering to education, music, art and design, it takes enormous courage and strength of character to risk a judgement that could potentially jeopardize their position at work. In time, our hope is that people become aware that frequently, many traits and behaviours that characterize Asperger's syndrome are the same traits and behaviours that enable those individuals to excel in their work lives.

A completely different set of traits and behaviours are required to form and maintain close personal relationships – and it is those traits and behaviours that are a challenge to individuals with AS. We hope that this book becomes a useful resource within those neurodiverse relationships.

Neurodiverse Relationships is a collection of writing from different people, some AS and some NT, each with a different style of writing. We are presenting the chapters as they've been written, in the authors' unique voice. Although we have tried to make the format 'flow' as much as possible, we felt it important to give continuation without diminishing the originality and authenticity of each of the contributors. To make the chapters completely uniform in style would defeat the purpose of the book – to give real voices an opportunity to speak. This book is about partnerships and the trials, the triumphs, different personalities, different topics and different approaches within them.

1

Anxiety

Anxiety

WINNIE'S STORY

From the beginning I knew John was moody. But he was very good-looking and intelligent, so I rose to the challenge! Before we were married I always felt like he had the upper hand but, because I was smitten with him, I stuck with it. Gradually, as I see it now, I lost myself in the process of trying to make him happy. The bad moods were stressful for both of us but because I was, and am, sensitive, I often felt hurt and anxious because it always felt like I was in the wrong – that I must have done something to displease him.

To get rid of some anxiety I constantly tried to please, and this manifested itself in the way I dressed, the way I looked, the way I spoke and the way I ate. At first I felt inferior because I came from a rough-and-tumble working-class family and lived in a council house. John was middle-class and from an academic family. They all had private education. His father was a university lecturer in classics. My father was a painter and decorator. It seemed like it was necessary for me to fit in with his family and not the other way round. He was often critical and sarcastic. The whole family were. They could be very witty and funny but also very cutting. I often felt that they were direct to the point of rudeness, but then I thought that's how 'posh' people were. So, by the time we got married I had changed from a fairly confident outgoing blond with lots of make-up and perfume to a plain Jane. In my sister's words, John took away her glamorous sister and I came back like an Amish woman!

All of this trying to please did nothing to stop John's bad moods, and I can see that, in some ways, I was actually afraid of him. He never shouted. He was never violent. He never threw things or slammed doors. He would just completely shut off from me. Very often he would go for a walk and then come back as if nothing had happened. Sadly, his mother died six months after our wedding and so I could not talk to her and ask what he was like as a child. His father was a very difficult man and possibly had Asperger's syndrome himself.

Because of my mother-in-law's sudden death I thought that John's apparent unhappiness in our first year of marriage was due to grief. When it continued, I put a lot of John's behaviour down to him being a repressed middle-class public school boy brought up in a male household: there were four boys and no sisters. His mother was lovely but not assertive, and so his father's excessive bad moods ruled the household. One son left and never came back. I found, in the early years, that it was a big mistake to ask John, 'What's the matter?' He hated it and became angry, so I imagine he felt anxious with my questions. His reactions made me feel anxious because I wanted to help him but felt rejected.

There seemed to be no displays of affection between the members of John's family. In fact, I often felt that they did their best to avoid each other. One brother says they were brought up with 'loving neglect'. My family was just the opposite. It was open house to friends and extended family. Everything was out in the open. If you got up in a bad mood someone would say, 'What's the matter with you? Get out of bed the wrong side?' Whereas in John's family home there were bad atmospheres and people kept away from my father-in-law because he seemed so formidable. Yet he also did not shout or throw things, he just used to have a face like thunder and people were wary of him.

This is the background to our early life together. In fact, I married someone I did not know at all well. He had been in the merchant navy for over three years so we only saw each other sporadically. When we married, he decided to leave the sea and get a shore job. In the early years, money was a problem. He came to the marriage with his father's attitude that all women were spendthrifts and kept a tight rein on the finances. This caused stress and anxiety because I was forever worrying about slipping up and spending when I shouldn't. He had a routine of going through the cheque book once a month with a little notebook while he tried to balance our finances. Every time he did it he would get in a bad mood, which made me very anxious. I now know that it was because he couldn't put finances in perspective. For him the glass was always half empty. He needed to save in order to feel secure and did as his father insisted and got a job with a good pension. This is one area in our 47-year marriage which has changed completely in that he now trusts me and feels more secure about money.

I lived as frugally as possible and luckily was very good with my hands, so I made my own clothes as well as the children's, when they came along. In fact, I was a very good housekeeper and shopped around for food. Everything was homemade if possible. I felt the shadow of my father-in-law also watching out for me being 'a typical woman' in his eyes.

His father's advice about getting a good pension affected us all as a family because John felt compelled to do well and climb the ladder so that his salary would rise, thus ensuring a good pension. He felt that this was the best thing he could do for us as a family at the time, but it meant that he was often away from home when we needed him most. His coming and going did not seem to affect him emotionally, to the point that it often felt that he had cut himself off from me and the children. My unhappiness about this must have puzzled him and made him wonder what he was doing wrong. It was always hard to explain to him the reason why I was upset. Very often he made decisions without any input from me. It was a long time before I had the courage to challenge him and question the rights and wrongs of some of these decisions. Ultimately, he learned that we needed to talk things over together. He thought he had been doing that but he had not. He comes across as very authoritative and strong-minded so I often felt anxious and weakened by what he did, and helpless and hopeless.

One of the traits of John's family was that they were all extremely pedantic. I had never come across this before. They corrected grammar and pronunciation all the time. I was bright at school but failed the 11+ so I had a bit of an inferiority complex about my education. I became nervous every time I was corrected for getting something wrong. This I would call anxiety now. When I decided to fight back I told them that they were in the wrong; that they were so busy looking at spelling and grammar mistakes they didn't ever get the real message. I used the analogy of receiving a letter or telegram bearing either very good or very bad news. I used to say that if a word was spelled wrong or the sentence wasn't grammatical they would only notice the mistakes and would not get the feelings, either good or bad – it would be the mistake that would matter. I can see why now but I couldn't understand it at the time. I get anxious when I am corrected by John's pedantry, especially in front of other people. I also get anxious when I feel he has said something inappropriate to a family member or friend.

In the early years of our marriage I did my best to fit in with John's wishes in the way that we lived. He had friends he had grown up with so he was not a complete loner. When they married we all became friends together so we did have a shared social life. In that respect it was good for our children in that we could go on holidays together and so all the children grew up together. But we had to move around the country with John's job. At one point I remember saying that we should make some friends. He snapped my head off, saying 'I've already got my friends'. So, I made my own friends and have been grateful for them.

Ten years after we got married I became chronically ill with ME. This had a major impact on all of the family as I struggled to live with it. Very often I felt that John was uncaring and can only now see that it was because he was finding life so stressful. I began to recognize his bad moods as depression and not as Asperger's syndrome because I hadn't heard of it. We kept up that belief for many years because depression seemed to be rife in John's family. It now seems that it is part and parcel of having AS, because depression can come about when John feels that he's done his best but has still got it wrong. As he says, 'I feel that I messed up again'.

My health problems have caused a lot of anxiety for both of us but, after 35 years, we have worked out ways of living with my ME and his AS. For the past five years I have also developed an eye condition and need to go to the eye clinic every month. This has been a worry to both of us because we do not know how bad my sight will get.

As for our life together now – occasionally things go wrong. It is usually when we have processed information differently so that he thinks we're doing one thing and I think we're doing something else. I feel that everything has to be spelled out to him. On a daily basis he likes to know what time a visitor is coming, what time my appointment at the hospital is, what time we are going out and so on. He will ask the same question several times. I imagine that the not knowing is stressful for him and that he needs my reassurance. I have to be patient and just repeat the times and not get cross about it and say 'I've already told you'. That's not helpful.

I get anxious when we start out on a journey and he immediately starts to criticize other drivers. His usual line is 'What are you doing?' in an impatient way to the driver in front of us. The driver can't hear, it's all very low-key but for me it starts an atmosphere of negativity just when I am anticipating a nice trip out and I get knots in my tummy.

I get anxious having to ask for things to be done for me all the time. John is my only carer and sometimes he gets impatient no matter how I word the request. At times it feels that he is snapping my head off when I have asked him to do something that will only take a minute. When I get upset about it he can now recognize this, which can cause anxiety for him but we are now much better at talking it through. I wish I didn't have to ask him for anything, but he is not always good at anticipating other people's needs.

I use an electric wheelchair most of the time indoors and out, but when I have to use a manual wheelchair I find it stressful when John is pushing me. He goes through the world as if everyone is in his way, and I feel very uncomfortable in places where there are crowds and I worry about the wheelchair banging into people's ankles. I feel disconnected from John behind me, and if things go wrong I have to get him to stop and come round and face me so that I can make eye contact to tell him how I feel. This has been and can still be one of our most anxiety-producing activities.

In the past I used to find it very difficult to ask John to take me anywhere because we didn't have an adapted car. That meant he had to dismantle my wheelchair and load it into the back of the car. I always felt I was being a nuisance to him as he is not good at giving reassuring remarks. Eventually we got an adapted car and this has helped. Even so, I don't think John likes giving lifts to anyone. He is independent and would not want to rely on anyone else for getting around. There are other situations where John's silence makes me feel anxious. When I told him I had just been given bad news about my eyes he didn't offer one word of comfort and when I have felt we were in dangerous or difficult situations, his silence makes it worse. Even though I have learned to understand it and he has tried to explain it, I still find his silences difficult to deal with.

Intimacy has always been a difficult subject for us to talk about and one that I feel John avoids, so I feel anxious about that. This was especially the case in the early years of our marriage.

JOHN'S STORY

I get anxious about phone calls; visitors who are not family; crowds in shops; waiting in queues; unwanted noise; getting too hot; having to appear as myself (rather than as an actor); getting things wrong; meeting strangers; finances occasionally but not so much as in the past; having to organize people and my wife, Winnie's, health, especially her eye problems. One of the worst parts of that is the endless waiting in hospital. I have found a way to cope with it by listening to French lessons. When the treatment first started it was horrendous for Winnie. I was able to hold her hand when she had eye injections, but I was not good at taking her mind off it during the waiting period because I felt overloaded myself with so many people around, bright lights and not knowing what was going to happen next. Winnie's anxiety would increase because I didn't know what to say to her. Her way of coping now is to have audio books to listen to.

I also feel anxious when there is a change of plan. Sometimes this is because I set an agenda for myself for the jobs I want to do on a given day and then Winnie asks me to do something else. I also feel anxious when she wants to bring other people in to do work in the house or garden. I would much rather do it myself because I like to keep busy, but also because I don't want strangers in my house.

Sometimes I feel anxious when Winnie wants to talk about feelings or incidents or actions that have upset her. I usually say that I don't know why I've done or said something. Nowadays she gives me time to think about an answer and then I come back to her with an explanation. Our communication about such incidents has improved greatly since I was assessed for AS.

I cannot always be spontaneous and feel anxious if that's what's expected of me. I also feel anxious when I am in a situation where I am expected to show feelings in the same way as other people, such as at funerals. I would much rather read a eulogy than sit amongst the bereaved.

Anticipating social events makes me anxious. Winnie is very gregarious but because of her illness/disability she needs me to accompany her. Sometimes I feel uncomfortable, but other times I can cope with it and begin to relax; it depends on the occasion and the people. I dislike small talk or being asked questions about myself. Now that Winnie understands about the AS she will often say that I can leave the event if I want to and is happy for me to take and fetch her. She can usually spot when I am uncomfortable and suggests I go outside for some fresh air or that I leave and come back later.

Sometimes journeys cause anxiety because I find that I have to concentrate very hard when I'm driving which I find very tiring. Winnie doesn't like the silence and sometimes there can be an atmosphere between us, especially when we have trouble reaching our destination. I also get anxious looking for parking spaces.

Since I retired 20 years ago I have a weekly day to myself when I go walking. Most of the time I go on a Wednesday when Winnie has someone in to help with household chores. I don't need any company when I am walking and I feel better for the exercise and the fresh air. Because of Winnie's eye treatment the Wednesday routine sometimes goes awry if she has an appointment on that day, but I have now learned to adjust as she always tells me that it's OK to go on another day. I feel tense if I cannot go at all.

I also took up amateur dramatics after I retired and this has helped with the anxiety and depression. This is something which I feel I can do with other people which doesn't make me feel uncomfortable. This is probably because I am playing a part rather than myself. Winnie is happy for me to do this hobby as we both get a social life from it and have made good friends. However, once again, this is affected by Winnie's health as it sometimes means leaving her by herself when she is ill.

I also play the guitar which I find relaxing but, when I am in a low mood, I feel that I will never be any good at it. Sometimes the guitar playing can cause stress or anxiety between me and Winnie because she feels shut out. In the early years of her illness I played it a lot and regularly shut myself away in another room, even though she had spent the day by herself. I didn't realize how lonely she felt or why it upset her. She found it hard to explain then but when I play now it reminds her of a lonely past and she doesn't like it. We are learning to compromise.

Most of our anxious moments occur when Winnie has a bad relapse of ME because she then has to stay in bed and doesn't like to be left alone. After 35 years we have worked out how to handle this situation, but in the past it was often a cause of upset between us. I am anxious when I feel that I am doing my best as a carer and husband but then get criticized for getting something wrong. I can see, though, that it is difficult for Winnie to lose her independence and that it is irksome for her to be so reliant on me.

When Winnie had to start using a wheelchair we both found it stressful because she felt out of control and I didn't like pushing her through crowded places. This would make me very anxious, but Winnie would think I was getting irritable with her and the whole wheelchair business.

I know that I shut down sometimes and I feel anxious because I cannot find the words to describe how I feel, and this becomes harder when I am put under pressure to do so. Winnie sometimes tells me she just wants some 'words' when I am silent and she feels upset when I tell her I don't know what to say.

When Winnie showed me Tony Attwood's book which explained Asperger's syndrome to me for the first time, I felt a great sense of relief. I always felt I was on the outside looking in and now I understand why.

Tony Attwood's Commentary and Q&A

One thing that those with ASC are very good at is worrying. Sometimes, when I meet adults, their greatest challenge in life may not be the ASC but the anxiety, which is quite debilitating. And of course the level of anxiety affects the level of Asperger's syndrome.

Now, in this chapter, Winnie describes how she *'always felt like I was in the wrong – that I must have done something to displease him'*. This is where you have the risk of personalizing AS and the pendulum swinging completely the other way and demonizing the partner. The hope is that couples can find a middle ground and a degree of mutual understanding and compromise. But in the initial stages, it's as Winnie says, constantly *'trying to please'* with the Aspie often being critical and sarcastic. Winnie identifies that the whole family were this way and, if you look at the family of someone with AS, often this is where those AS characteristics have been expanded and, as far as the person is concerned, that's the style they know and that's what they want to introduce into their own family.

'Very often he would go for a walk and then come back as if nothing had happened.' Yes, there are times when the AS partner will disappear to resolve the issues but, back at home, those issues have not been resolved.

'I put a lot of John's behaviour down to being a repressed, middle-class, public school boy, brought up in a male household. There were four boys and no sisters.' Well yes, you've got a contextual explanation but it really doesn't explain everything. It does indicate that there was a very powerful patriarch there, probably Aspie as well, who seemed formidable. Again that's a controlling influence and being a bully or a 'domestic terrorist'.

'[T]hey were so busy looking at spelling and grammar mistakes they didn't ever get the real message.' There's a mind-set with AS that's really looking for patterns and errors and correcting them without

realizing how people will feel when their error is corrected. The person with AS can be left surprised that the person isn't thanking them for their error being pointed out! There's a lot of correction, but one of the areas that I have to work on with couples is compliments, and the view of 'Why should I give you a compliment about something you already know you're good at?' In relationship counselling I speak Aspergerese in terms of fighting Aspie with Aspie. I tell people 'You *must* give your wife two compliments a day. Here is a list of topics which you can compliment her about. This is the chart and you *must* give her two compliments a day.' Although it's a bit false, it's lovely for the partner to get the compliments. So, as much as the tendency is to criticize, the counter to that is that it's very rare to compliment. The AS partner may not understand that neurotypicals need compliments.

One of the things that Winnie mentions is depression, a sense of negativity. By nature, those with Asperger's tend to be pessimists, and there is a link between anxiety and depression. One of the risks of Asperger's syndrome in adults is cyclical depression. At least 80 per cent of those with Asperger's syndrome have constant debilitating anxiety. Up to 70 per cent will also have cyclical depression. Sometimes it's very deep, with suicidal thoughts or even suicidal actions. Dealing with someone who is clinically depressed is obviously going to affect the relationship irrespective of the ASC.

John describes feeling anxious when there is a change of plan, and this is because he has to recalibrate his brain to the new situation. He has his expectations and he's all prepared for that, that's the script; and when the script changes, the person with AS will feel very, very disturbed.

He describes how he would *'much rather read a eulogy than sit amongst the bereaved'*. Sometimes, at funerals, the person with Asperger's syndrome is thinking, 'Why are people crying? She reached a good age.' They don't realize that commonly, amongst neurotypicals, tears are infectious, but this is not necessarily so for Aspies.

John says in this chapter, *'I didn't realize how lonely she felt or why it upset her.'* If he can't see it, then it doesn't exist. This means that the neurotypical person has to be very forthright and explain, unemotionally, why they feel as they do – and what the AS partner can do to help.

Winnie talks about trying to make John happy. How far should the NT partner live their life trying to accommodate the anxieties and stresses of their AS spouse?

Well you can try and do that, but I don't think you can do it alone. You try and bring in professional help because if the anxiety and/or depression has reached the stage that it is having a significant effect on that person's quality of life then they need help from a psychologist or a psychiatrist.

Winnie talks about trying to make John happy. But really we need to explore the concept of happiness. What happens with neurotypicals is that they resonate with each other's happiness and infect each other with happiness. Now, you can infect an Aspie with negativity, which they will amplify and, by nature, they will tend to be pessimistic. However, they do not find it easy to absorb and resonate with other people's happiness. They have difficulty being 'jollied up'. Generally, people with AS experience happiness differently to neurotypicals. Someone with AS is more likely to find happiness in solitude, solving a problem, or spending time on their special interest... which is the ultimate happiness.

How common is it for the NT partner to be 'Aspergated' (influenced by Asperger traits to such an extent that they begin to take on these traits themselves)? How can this be prevented?

Yes, it is absolutely a case of Asperger's is infectious and, if you can't beat 'em, join 'em. Often the first tendency is to accommodate, to create an Aspie-friendly environment in which the Aspie will flourish, but eventually, within this, the NT does not flourish. So again it's a question of sacrifice, and finding a middle-ground.

What can a person with AS do to ease their anxiety? Is the relationship itself a cause of anxiety in an NT/AS relationship?

I think there are many causes for the anxiety and depression, but one of them can actually be the relationship. There is depression at not meeting the NT partner's needs: 'I know he/she is miserable and unhappy and that I'm contributing to that, but I don't know how or why and so I don't know what to do to bring him/her out of it.' This is an area that needs to be addressed with an AS-aware counsellor because there is a high level of depression in both partners when one of the partners has the characteristics of Asperger's syndrome. So failure in some areas of the relationship can affect the Aspie too and can be a cause of their depression.

Is pedantry linked to Asperger's?
Yes, of course. A feature of Asperger's syndrome is seeing the detail rather than the big picture. This can be very useful in certain work settings but incredibly debilitating within a relationship or social context. The person with AS is also, by nature, likely to be pessimistic, which is fed by the need to point out others' errors.

John talks about feeling a 'sense of relief' when he read your book and understood that he had AS. How important is a diagnosis/self-awareness when dealing with AS-related anxiety?
It's very important, not just to the person with AS but also to the therapist, so that they can modify their treatment according to the Aspie 'culture' and way of thinking. And of course it can be very helpful to the neurotypical in providing understanding of their partner's behaviour.

2

Change

DAVID'S STORY

Change has implications on two levels.

Superficially, for the Aspie trying to remain hidden in plain sight by putting on an act of perceived normality, change is the enemy of good planning. We spend a significant proportion of our energies trying to organize things so that we can sail through life unimpeded by having to make split-second decisions based on the emotional states of others. We do this by planning out nearly all of the courses of action that could be taken across a whole range of circumstances so that we are ready for anything any neurotypical might throw at us. Except, of course, change itself.

I find that neurotypicals love change: change the wallpaper, get a new car, move the furniture. This can infuriate us Aspies. We have just got used to the old layout of the house, now you want us to have to memorize a new one. But I suppose that change and organizing things the way that you want them is inevitable – it's a fundamental law of physics – disorder always increases, or something like that.

However, it's the second type of change – a slow creeping change in the status of a relationship – that concerns me.

I believe that, like lots of Aspies, I set out to find, woo and secure a partner. This formed part of my bigger plan to hide in plain sight by appearing somehow normal to the world. My peer group all had long track records of seeking boyfriends and girlfriends and eventually pairing off, and I had to do the same.

I'm not sure if I was lucky or unlucky; I found Karen very quickly after starting the search in earnest. No ill-fated fumbles at university, just rescuing other people's drunken girlfriends from cubicles they had locked themselves into and fallen asleep. One incident of mumbling 'Do you want to go for a drink after work?' to a girl miles out of my league, with a thankfully short but gentle let-down. One no-show to an answer to a small ad that pre-dated internet dating. And then I met Karen at work, and we just sort of clicked. Workmates cajoled me to take her out. I worked hard to woo; to act as 'neurotypically' as I felt able. I guess that probably came across as a mix of nervousness and chivalry, possibly even generosity. We married – the best party either of us had ever planned or attended – surrounded by friends; naysayers weren't invited!

But then change kicked in. I think I would have been comfortable to maintain the status quo almost indefinitely, but Karen, as a neurotypical, wanted change – and frequently. And, I discovered, relationship change is much more complicated than furniture-layout change.

Karen didn't know I was an Aspie and neither, really, did I. At primary school I had been seen by an educational psychologist, but this pre-dated the drive in the UK for Asperger's diagnoses and my behaviour had been poles apart from 'classic' autism. The matter slid; I moved on into adulthood undiagnosed, oblivious.

We soon bought a pet, but things didn't work out the way that Karen had expected. She thought I would enjoy Dylan the dog's company as much as she did, but here was relationship change – I was competing for Karen's affection with a cute Welsh Springer and I was losing out. Dylan's affection was almost unconditional – just food and walks; mine came with a hefty bundle of strings attached. The dog's tolerance only served to emphasize my demands.

I'm of working-class stock, pulled up by my own boot-straps to lower-middle with my university education and world-travelling engineering job. Karen was from an upper-middle background and wanted me to operate and socialize at that level. I think Karen started to realize I was different, odd, perhaps a bit broken when I failed to respond favourably to keeping up the correct act at social gatherings – both intimate and full-scale parties. I hated dressing up and talking about the weather with near strangers. My social cup has always filled up quickly.

Set against this change, I had a constant in my life: my obsession or special interest was my work, my job, my career. I think Karen might have resented how much I threw into my job. Karen was probably disappointed that having been herself a 'special project' (a shorter-term obsession) she was now vying to be my current obsession with something in my life that was almost as important as her.

I'd tried to get the vicar to miss out the bit about having children, but he slipped it back in between the draft and the delivery of the marriage vows. It seemed to be a biological imperative and the right social thing to do, so along came more change with the entries into the world of our son and daughter. This change felt like a trap. I am hypersensitive to bodily fluids so it was no good me trying to change a nappy. I think that, with a touch of post-natal depression, came disappointment from Karen that I wasn't joining in with the work of child-rearing. Instead I looked forward to the days when I would be able to help my kids with their homework.

So I think it very much appeared to Karen that our relationship went greatly downhill after marriage. I'm not sure whether I didn't notice this bad change (in which case I appeared oblivious) or if I somehow didn't consider the change to have been significant (in which case I appeared inconsiderate).

And here I come to my central thrust on the question of change in a relationship. How do you measure relationship 'success' in the face of change? Indeed, what is the neurotypical definition of 'success' in a marriage? Is it somehow 'lasting' to the 25th anniversary when the kids have left home and the parents are still together? Or is it that the couple should be as loving, amorous and sexually active as when they were courting? Could a successful outcome become two people enjoying life but somewhat more separately than they were at the beginning of their relationship; just good friends? Or something in between all of the above? Just how do you benchmark the quality of a relationship?

Was the time around our son's diagnosis with Asperger's the lowest ebb of our relationship? Very probably. Karen instigated a very big change that was ultimately beneficial in starting to study to become much more educated about Asperger's. Along the way she unofficially diagnosed me with those apples of my son and daughter not falling far from the paternal tree. There were also some signs amongst her family. The big changes – formalizing my coping strategies as being those of an Aspie, studying them and starting to document our relationship for her Master's thesis.

Perhaps we are part way through tearing our relationship down and rebuilding it stronger with a mutual understanding.

Both Karen and I have been taking more of an interest in how other couples' relationships pan out; especially when one or other of the couple is an Aspie. There does seem to be an awful lot of relationship failure, often catalysed by changes, and very small changes at that.

But back to my central concern on relationship change. I believe, admittedly on scant evidence, that lots of wholly neurotypical-to-neurotypical relationships fail when faced with change, but also many fail through a *lack* of change and progression. Where is that happy medium? What hope for the Aspie marriage where one party is allergic to change? Is there some comfort down the route of marriage guidance counselling? Seemingly not in the UK where, through a lack of specialist counsellors that understand both conventional relationships and the contrasting thought patterns and behaviours of Aspies, conventional wisdom might be that the couple should never have had a relationship in the first place and perhaps it might be better if it broke down amicably. And there's another obstacle to conventional marriage counselling – I've carefully constructed the persona that I believe my neurotypical cohort of friends and Karen want to see and I don't want some relationship counsellor to go probing amongst its foundations undermining it, decomposing it to demonstrate a lie.

So I want to undertake the right amount of relationship change, some would call it relationship growth, but I need to measure my progress. Karen had a few relationships before meeting up with me and, as a result, has something to measure me against. I didn't have any failed or successful relationships before Karen, so I don't have the benefit of a benchmark.

And I don't think a multiple choice pop-quiz in *Cosmopolitan* – 'How strong is your relationship?' – is quite going to suffice. I need proper cutting-edge social science.

KAREN'S STORY

When we met I was going through a lot of change. I had just left university and literally a couple of days before David asked me out had dumped my long-term serious boyfriend of six years. This was the person I had expected to marry, and the feeling had been reciprocated, but in the last year he had gone off to university as a mature student and the freedom had gone to his head. I was devastated and angry, but I was not one to sit at home and mope. I had student debts to pay and having a job to do kept my mind off my woes somewhat.

I joined a temping agency and ended up at this strange engineering company in deepest darkest Newcastle on the edge of the Tyne. I was a little nervous about starting, but David was one of the first people I spoke to and he went out of his way to make me comfortable. The company was full of educated engineers – all men, the only women were the admin staff. I have always been a tomboy, being brought up with two brothers and many close male friends, and I felt completely at home. I was happy to sit and chat with the engineers at breakfast and lunch. Perhaps my joining in with the men was taken as flirting, but I chatted and laughed with them all equally. David was one of them.

Unbeknownst to me, as we sat having coffee on the lawn, David actually entering sunlight was unheard of. So there's the first change he made for me: he downed tools and made an effort to make social contact. I didn't notice anything odd, but this change was closely observed by his colleagues and, especially, by the women. One girl in particular who was the same age as me took my home phone number and passed it on to David and instructed him to ring me.

I was a little surprised at the communication but thought 'Why not?' I moved in with him within a month and stayed for a year before I got my dream job in London. He treated me like a princess, and who wouldn't like that?

Fast forward two years and we were married with a baby on the way. It is true that we told the vicar that we didn't want children and, at that moment in time, neither of us was mentally prepared for them. I knew what it was like to have a baby in the house as my sister arrived as a little surprise when I was 16. After the initial shock she was loved and adored by all of us, but I observed how tired my mum was, and I wasn't ready for that yet. I'd only just started on my career. However, something changed – apparently only in me although I thought it was a joint decision – and I got pregnant. David was wonderful during the pregnancy, very supportive and loving, and even during the labour I couldn't have asked for anything more. But he completely changed before we even got Morgan home from hospital. He was very rude to my mother and extremely anxious around me and the baby. I thought it only natural so didn't worry about it at first.

As time went on I found the baby very hard work. He didn't sleep, he didn't feed. I've just discovered that David thought I had post-natal depression – I really didn't. I had the baby-blues on day four as most mums do. I was tired and obviously David wasn't the focus of my attention any more. You'd think if he thought I was actually depressed he would have suggested I get some help. He never did. I did lose my temper with him massively one day. His idea of helping me not be so tired was to move into the spare bedroom. I went berserk! I felt rejected, unsupported and unloved. He was terrified of me as I started throwing things, and he decided that moving rooms wasn't a good idea after all. That moment was pivotal for me. I didn't often lose my temper but I was at my lowest ebb and he had just tipped me over the cliff. However, I saw the fear and confusion in his eyes and I stopped. I calmed myself down. I try and walk away now when he is winding me up, as I know I am the only one that can stop the situation getting worse. I changed that day. In some ways I grew up but I wonder if I lost a bit of my personality. Perhaps I sacrificed standing up for myself in order to keep a happy household for my little family.

We've now been married 18 years and our eldest child is 16. He also has Asperger's syndrome but getting to know and understand my son as he grows has helped me to know, understand and tolerate David a lot more. I see my son in him, especially when he is bewildered.

I have to stamp on my own spontaneity regularly so as not to invoke too much change in our home. I love change. It is fresh and exciting, but to them it can be confusing or even terrifying. We now plan change as much as we can, but sometimes life just happens.

For example, we both work from home, so one day I suggested, as the kids were at school and it was lunchtime that we should pop out for lunch. The mention of food is always welcome and is the one thing I can be spontaneous about with David! He thought it was a great idea. We got ready to leave the house when I had an idea. We had been cutting the hedge and had a load of rubbish to take to the local tip, which was on the way. I suggested my brilliant idea of killing two birds with one stone, thinking he would immediately realize it would save us two trips, but no. He had the most enormous strop and was most disagreeable. I quickly realized my mistake and tried to backtrack, saying I would go another time. However, I had already put the thought in his head and he knew that this was what I wanted or I wouldn't have suggested it. He wouldn't let me back down and insisted on putting all the rubbish in the car with bad grace and driving to the tip. The atmosphere over lunch was horrendous. I wished I'd never opened my mouth. I try to think more than one step ahead these days. It's quite exhausting at times, especially when you are always the one at fault.

As mentioned by my dear husband, changing the furniture is a big issue for him! My mother used to move furniture around all the time. I would come home from school and the dining room would have moved into the conservatory and the study into the front room. I didn't mind a bit. I'm not sure how my dad felt about this. To me, furniture is not fixed to the floor so why shouldn't it move around? It gives the room a new feeling without having to decorate and helps with a thorough spring clean.

The first time I did this was a complete surprise to David, and he never lets me forget it. I used to come home from work a few hours before him as, unlike him, I stuck to my office hours.

I decided to rearrange the room as it hadn't changed since the day I moved in and I felt I could organize it better. Later, when he walked through the door, he just stood there paralysed, apart from his mouth, which was opening and closing silently. I knew then I had done something wrong. He insisted we change it back there and then. At the time I thought that maybe I had stepped over some invisible line with it being his house that I had moved into. Now I know that if I had given him advance warning and a set of detailed plans he would have let me do it.

Of course this makes moving house a complete nightmare. Again, I love change and I love moving house – a change is as good as a rest! I must be so annoying to him. And yet we'd still be in that tiny little starter home now if I hadn't insisted we needed more room. When we do move house you might expect there to be great discussions about where the furniture will go but no, it is all being worked out in his head or drawn up with little scaled sofas on his CAD package. He doesn't trust my instincts and imagination at all. I'm usually right when I say a piece of furniture will fit in a certain place, but he only remembers the times I am wrong. To me, if I am wrong we move it back or try somewhere else. What's the big deal?

The other major issue is when we change cars. This wasn't much of an issue when we first married as I didn't drive and didn't have an opinion. In the last twelve years however, especially since our little business has contract hire cars, both of which need to be changed every three years, this has caused massive problems.

For a start he has low self-esteem so whenever we went to the more prestige car showrooms he would be very rude to the sales people or, if we were ignored, he would march out in disgust vowing never to go back. He doesn't seem to understand the concept of window-shopping, and, though sales people would love to sell to everyone who walks into their showroom, they know the likelihood of a sale is low. Also David seems to think that if I say I like a car what I'm really saying is that I must have it there and then. He can't relax and enjoy himself, despite the fact he actually loves cars and anything to do with them.

Our most expensive purchase through the company was an Audi. Unbeknownst to me, David had always hankered after an Audi. You would never have guessed as he spent a lot of his driving time insulting Audi drivers and criticizing what he saw as their aggressive driving styles. This turned out to be his reaction to thinking he wasn't good enough for an Audi. After a massive strop when he had walked out of a showroom because he felt we were being ignored, he sent a letter of complaint to the manager. He actually received a very polite phone call back though unfortunately the manager reinforced David's fears. He admitted that his sales teams were trained to look out for likely looking clients and ignore those who they deemed not serious. I pointed out that the people most likely to be able to afford an expensive car were not the ones dressed up to the nines on a Saturday, but those who weren't outwardly trying to prove their means. The manager agreed. He then arranged for David and me to come in for an appointment and arranged for the exact cars that we were interested in to be there to look at.

All well and good you might say. We ordered the car David liked (I got to choose the colour, which he didn't care about as long as it wasn't flashy red) and we waited for it to be delivered. On the day we were due to collect the car we took the children who were very excited. The plan was to drive down in one car and drive back in two. I would drive the old car. It took ages for the car to be handed over and David had to sit in the car with the salesman for about 40 minutes while he explained how everything worked. The children and I stood outside all the while. When we eventually left, David immediately stalled the car, which I think annoyed him. By the time we got back home he decided he hated the car and was never going to drive it again. This was exactly the same car as the one he had test driven and loved.

He didn't get on with the new handbrake and didn't trust it. I drove the car, a little nervously at first, but soon got the hang of it. He would sit in the passenger seat instructing me on what to do as he had had the lesson on how to work everything. He would tell me how wonderful it was in one breath and in the next that he would never drive it. This was very stressful, and his mood at home was very low and irritable. Eventually after a few weeks he got bored of being a passenger and decided to give the car 'another chance'. He was more relaxed having seen me cope with it, and because he believes he is a better driver than me this would have irked him. He was still very anxious about driving it but he started to trust it a little. We then made the bad decision to take a 600-mile round trip to London and home via Liverpool. He wasn't too bad on the way down, but on the day we were driving back he received a phone call from work that really upset him and he became very aggressive towards other drivers. After we had visited his sister in Liverpool his behaviour became increasingly worse. He became paranoid that everyone on the road was out to get him. He was driving home in the dark along the motorway at 40 miles an hour. I was terrified as it was way too slow for a motorway and I was convinced we would cause an accident, especially as the weather was terrible. He wouldn't stop and let me drive but at the same time he was gibbering and tearful. There was nothing I could do but stay outwardly calm. If I tried to make any suggestions, he bit my head off or started freaking out. I was terrified for our and the children's lives. If I even moved a hand or a leg, he took it as criticism and screamed at me. I didn't know what to do and did the only thing I could, which was to scrape my nails up my arm and back down again, making it red raw. It was the only relief I had. I thought the journey would never end, and I seriously thought I would have to call out an emergency mental health team if we ever got home.

We've had the car for over two years now and most of the time he is fine with it. He still doesn't like the handbrake, and I can tell when he is anxious as his driving gets erratic again but not to the same extent. We have started to look around for a new car, but I'm hoping that now he is used to being an Audi driver he is a little more confident and that this time will be easier for both of us.

Tony Attwood's Commentary and Q&A

I love how David describes his attitude to change in his first paragraph: 'We spend a significant proportion of our energies trying to organize things so that we can sail through life unimpeded by having to make split-second decisions based on the emotional states of others.' For people with Asperger's syndrome, change and surprises are extremely stressful. It threatens to tear down all the careful planning and organizing that helps an Aspie impose some order and control on their world.

Difficulty coping with change and interrupted routines is one of the core diagnostic characteristics of autism. And yet I think, by and large, people associate this trait with autistic children. They can forget that autistic children become autistic adults, with all the same traits and challenges. Adults with AS may find some coping strategies to learn to manage change better, but their issues with inflexibility are still there – they don't easily 'grow out of it'. As neurotypical adults living in an ever-changing world where we adapt daily to all kinds of circumstances without even thinking about it, this kind of rigidity can be very difficult to understand and even more difficult to live with.

David brings up a valid point – that of how relationship 'success' is measured in the face of change. Relationships do change over time and, in the case of an NT/AS relationship, it is up to the couple themselves to determine what works for them and what both partners are happy with, rather than feeling they must measure their relationship against the world's benchmark for 'success'.

David talks about being 'allergic to change'. Is this aversion to change biological? A direct result of a person's Asperger's syndrome?
It isn't always easy to determine whether a person's need for routines and rigidity comes directly from their AS or from the anxiety linked to their AS. Either way, what we do know is that dealing with a change of plan or changes in circumstances is hugely stressful where AS is concerned. Routines make life more predictable and therefore more

manageable for the person with Asperger's syndrome. Without the skills of intuition or adaptation to help them, the Aspie needs to know what lies ahead and prepare themselves in advance for events. If a plan changes, it causes huge stress for the Aspie. Surprises, chaos and uncertainty are to be avoided at all costs. This is possible, to a certain extent, when the Aspie is single. The problems arise within the context of a relationship and a family, when keeping life predictable becomes harder.

Karen talks about how supportive and loving David was during her pregnancy but describes him completely changing before they'd even got the baby home from hospital. Can you explain this?
Yes. It's change again. While Karen was pregnant, the baby wasn't there yet. Life hadn't had to change very much. As we all know, when a baby comes along, everything changes. For the person with ASD this is incredibly stressful. Their dependence on routines often increases during times of change and yet, right at the time that David needed routine and regularity the most, everything was changing and out of his control.

Why did David react so badly to something as minor as taking a quick detour to the tip on the way to lunch?
Because it wasn't in his plan of what was about to happen. He hadn't had time to process it. It was a change and the instinctive reaction for an Aspie is to resist change because it threatens your sense of order, the way you keep the world under control.

When a plan changes, even slightly, it requires the person with Asperger's to recalibrate their brain to this new situation. David had his expectations, he was all prepared for one thing and that's the script – and then the script changes. This will make the Aspie feel very disturbed.

Anxiety, for the Aspie, is heightened by worrying about something that could happen that's unpleasant, so they become controlling to try to avoid that from happening. If a plan changes, this control is taken away from them and the anxiety builds up again.

Karen talks about how she always seems to be the one at fault, in David's opinion. Why is this?

It's the Aspie's Teflon coating – 'nothing sticks on me'. It's their comforting mechanism throughout their life for having made so many errors. The arrogance comes from a need to self-comfort, especially with intellect: 'I'm superior to other people.' It's the classic line in *The Imitation Game* where Alan Turing is being bullied and teased. He's got a friend, Christopher, and they're talking about Alan being bullied and Alan Turing says, 'They bully me because I'm smarter than they are.' Christopher replies, 'No, it's because you're different.' But Alan's perception is that it is due to his greater intelligence. Because, if you're not good socially and you're not good at sport, the only thing you've got is your intelligence. So that becomes your comfort, it becomes your arrogance and the way you perceive life. When people are stupid that is an insult to your precious intelligence and so it's almost impossible to admit that you've done something stupid. So you over-fixate on intellect or the thing that you are good at and judge everyone else against this. It is not being different, it is being superior.

This can also impact families with children whereby the AS parent may tend to measure their children's ability purely on their intellect and how well they're doing at school, rather than whether the child is happy in school.

David states that he thinks it appeared to Karen that their relationship went downhill after marriage. Is this common in an AS/NT relationship?

The Aspie may give everything to a relationship during courtship – as David himself describes, the other person becomes their special interest. Of course this devotion is very appealing to the person on the receiving end, but it takes a huge amount of effort from the person with AS and cannot be maintained. One of the things common to many NT/AS partnership is that, after marriage, everything changes. In this instance, the change is brought on by the AS partner. It's almost as though the person has won the prize and they don't have to put in any effort any more. 'You've signed the contract, that's it, I no longer need to pretend.'

Karen describes how she changed the day that she lost her temper with David. She describes growing up but also losing a bit of her personality. Whereas the partner with AS resists change, is it necessary for the NT partner to embrace change in themselves in order to accommodate the AS partner and to keep life calm? How can the NT partner make sure they don't lose themselves in the process?

Yes, to a certain extent, the NT partner will have to change to adapt to life with an AS spouse. It's a very real issue though that the NT partner, if they are not careful, can start to change in ways that they don't want to, just to keep the peace. They begin to mirror the traits of their AS spouse and so they might, for example, avoid change, or stop socializing. Asperger's is infectious one-way – you hope, as an NT, that you are going to change the Aspie. No. If you did that, you would get the Nobel Prize for science and peace! The change comes from the other direction, and so it's very important that the NT partner has a social life with other NTs to re-establish who they were prior to the AS relationship – to rediscover the things that made them happy. It's important to have time without your partner whether it's a night out, an opportunity to be with people, to laugh, to be silly or frivolous, to metaphorically 'let your hair down'. It's that opportunity to feel gloriously NT again – to go back to your own 'culture'. Because being in relationship with someone with Asperger's syndrome, is like being a foreigner in a different land – and you need to go back to your own culture to remind yourself of who you are in order to be true to yourself. Maintaining and regularly seeing NT friends is better than Prozac – you can quote me on that!

David identifies a lack of 'specialist counsellors' for AS/NT marriages in the UK. Do you think this is a problem?

Yes it is. Traditional relationship counselling is about 'how do you feel?' For the NT, that is your language, you understand it, you know how you feel and you can articulate this. But for an Aspie, they often don't know how they feel. They don't know what's going through their mind. They know there are lots of feelings there but they can't put words to them. So it is very important that you find a counsellor who is knowledgeable and trained in counselling for people on the spectrum and, specifically, the relationship issues that arise from an NT/AS relationship. A counsellor with that level of experience and training is hard to find.

Communication

ALICE'S STORY

I am not the sort of person who spends a long time wrapping presents. I usually manage to disguise them in some way so there is some sense of 'opening'. On a bad day this might be under a jumper. On a better day I will have found some wrapping paper (possibly pre-used) and some tape and managed to combine these in a way that creates something that looks like it might be a gift. I'm not one of those people for whom present wrapping is an art form, where the ribbon and paper coordinate and the package looks perfect. Some say this is because I am disorganized. Some say it's because I don't care. Maybe it's because I am too busy. But surely what is important is the gift inside the wrapping.

Sometimes Ben's communication is not packaged in a socially acceptable way. Sometimes he shouts. Sometimes he does not respond at all. I can take offence at the way his communication is wrapped (or the fact he didn't wrap it at all!) – I don't like being shouted at or ignored. If his communication is different to what I am used to, I can become fearful. Is he going to hurt me? Is he going to leave me?

I am learning to look for the underlying message rather than get distracted by the unusual delivery. It means taking a moment to pause (or sometimes a few moments) rather than jumping to conclusions. It means winding back and looking for good intentions. It means remembering what the lived experience can be like for someone on the autistic spectrum.

Today when I turned on the vacuum cleaner, he shouted at me to turn it off. A few minutes earlier I had vacuumed near him with no problem. This caught me off guard, and my initial reaction was to criticize him for shouting at me as I found it unnecessarily rude. However, I managed to hold my tongue as I wondered whether his reaction was due to a sensory issue. A while later, when he was calmer, he explained that the sound had been more intense the second time round as it had bounced off the wall next to him and was affecting his concentration. The shouting wasn't logical – speaking in a normal voice would have had the same effect without the added complication of offence and the consequences that might entail. The shouting seemed to be an urgent desperate plea, which makes me wonder what the sound of the vacuuming actually felt like to him. I am starting to notice a link between Ben coming across as rude and his anxiety levels. Now that I am conscious of this, I try to put my judgements to one side and offer support for his anxiety.

There are other occasions when sensory experience can create unusual communication. For example, when he feels my cold hands or feet he screams! This gets his message across, but I am left with a raised heart rate! Sometimes it is more subtle – for example if we are in a crowded place I can notice him becoming quiet and looking around nervously. He doesn't need to tell me with words that he is anxious and wants to leave. I can notice his fast breathing and give him some options for a way forward.

Something called the traffic light exercise that we came across in a workbook for AS/NT partnerships has been really useful for us. This is a visual form of communication rather than words. The exercise invites the AS partner to write their own statements to link in with a colour to explain their feelings and identify their meltdown process ahead of time. We don't remember to identify whether he feels green, amber or red very often. However when I do notice him withdrawing or see him having a meltdown, I can remind myself of the positive and loving statements he made in his statements during the traffic light exercise and I find this very reassuring. What he wrote down in the workbook months ago, gives me the emotional support I need when we come to those situations.

I come from a family where communication is indirect and subtle; where other people's preferences are explored before your own are expressed. This works fine if everyone is doing it, but in my relationship with Ben I have needed to develop a more assertive and direct style. I have been learning to make my statements in a bold way so that they are noticed and get more of a response. It feels similar to writing a birthday card to a child who is learning to read; we make our letters larger and clearer so they are recognized rather than using our usual handwriting. It can feel a little exaggerated but it is more appropriate for the purpose.

At the same time, it has felt very awkward for me to try to adapt my communication style to one that is more direct, clear and assertive. I worry that when I am trying to stand up for myself I come across as nagging or needy. However this is preferable (I think) to the other option, which involves retreating into myself and becoming passive.

In contrast, Ben is completely comfortable with boldly asserting his needs to me. He has no hang-ups or emotional baggage. Often it turns out that his requests are not that important to him and he is quite happy to accept a negative response. He knows that I find it difficult to say no to him and will sometimes encourage me to refuse him.

At other times he is not quite so connected with how things are for me and I am left struggling to make a judgement on how to meet his demands and requests for favours, e.g. 'Will you make me a cup of tea?', 'Will you watch this clip on YouTube with me?' or 'Will you get the screwdriver from downstairs?' I can often end up feeling that I should prioritize his request even if it is not obviously important and he has not explained why he is asking. Should I trust him that he has a good reason for asking for my help? Should I just stop whatever I was doing? How should his needs and wants balance with mine? If he needs help then, of course, I want to be supportive and provide this. However, I also don't want to end up as his maid. When is it the right time for him to take responsibility for himself and when does he need a helping hand?

Since he is so free with asking, it is up to me to make the judgement call. It can be difficult to explore the situation surrounding the request. How are you feeling at the moment? What led to you asking me for help with this? What would be the benefit of my help? What would be the outcome if I refused? Usually, I can't find answers to these questions and am left trying to work out via clues (like body language, general stress level) how much he needs the help vs. the importance of what I was doing and my plan for the day.

Some of the things Ben says feel empty, fake and distant. They leave me feeling more alone than no response at all. Sometimes I choose not to start a conversation because if I don't get a real, connected response I can see it affecting my mood negatively. The gaps in between real communication can be lonely. There is no telling how long the withdrawal will be – a few minutes or a few weeks. Texting him can work very well as we are distanced from each other's emotional states. I can feel like there is a more genuine connection than when we are face to face.

The strange communication patterns that exist at home are in contrast to those that occur when we are out. Ben has thoroughly educated himself on social and communication theories and is a much more confident communicator than me when we are in social situations. He notices how social hierarchies work and is really good at making people feel included in social situations even though he finds it exhausting. He takes risks with how he interacts with people and has learned, through trial and error, what works. He is pretty expert and gives me tips and encouragement to stand up for myself in social situations.

In terms of what we want to communicate, I came up with the following categories, although there are probably more:

- Practicalities
- Long-term planning
- Emotional support
- Sensory experience
- Ritual communication
- Love for each other
- Special interest
- Extras.

Practicalities – e.g. 'Who is making dinner?', 'What are your plans at the weekend?', 'Your mum wants you to call her' or 'Please can you pick me up?'

I find this is best done via a text, app or short verbal statement. We have a shared calendar on our electronic devices, which is helpful, and we have just started using an app for sharing jobs around the home.

I find it useful to have a Plan B ready that does not need the input of my partner. Then, if the plan which involved him doesn't work out, I am not left feeling resentful or abandoned because I have another option that serves the purpose. For example, if there is a film I want to watch I might invite a few people to the cinema rather than relying on my AS partner to leave the house to come with me. Another example, as a result of Ben struggling to get me to the train station on time, is finding other ways of getting there that mean I don't have to rely on him. This planning ahead reduces both our stress levels and actually results in a higher level of involvement from him.

Long-term planning – e.g. 'Should we move house?' or 'Where should we spend Christmas?'

We find it best to talk about these sorts of things when we are both calm. For us this can mean when we are out at a favourite restaurant or on a long car journey. I would like to have these sorts of conversations while walking, but Ben prefers a more static conversation.

Emotional support – e.g. 'I had a bad day' or 'I got the job!'

This is the part of the relationship where we make ourselves especially vulnerable.

Ben has got better at recognizing my moods the longer we have been together, which is nice. If he finds me in a bad or strange mood, he often checks whether I am upset with him.

Ben supports me with all sorts of issues. He listens, gives me a hug and reassures me. He is very affirming of my character and my abilities. Sometimes I have to wait a while for this support because he is elsewhere (mentally). I liken this to airline passengers being told to fit their oxygen masks before helping other people. My partner needs to spend a lot of time adjusting his oxygen mask as it keeps slipping. It is right that he sorts this out first. I find that when I rush him and demand support when I need it, it is counterproductive because he isn't able to provide it and I end up feeling worse. It's better for me to wait until he is fully available. We have a saying at home which we both find very helpful. It is 'You do you'. It essentially means – look after yourself first – I can wait. I approach other people for support in the meantime. This can feel counter-intuitive when Ben is in the same room as me but I am getting better at it.

Sometimes he offers me advice in a way that I find unhelpful. The advice is very definite and he seems to be saying, 'This is the right way of doing things' or 'This is the only way forward'. I am trying to get better at recognizing when this is happening and the emotional impact it has on me. Sometimes I say that I am not looking for advice or solutions, so please don't give any. Sometimes I just change the subject to something else, depending on my energy levels.

Sensory experience – e.g. 'Turn it off!' or 'I don't feel well.'

This one is very closely related to emotional support. I think this is especially the case for Ben who, for a communication exercise, listed 'feeling cold' as one of ten emotions he experiences. He seems to have a hypersensitivity to his body in terms of pain, digestive processes and temperature.

Rituals – e.g. 'Good morning' when we wake up, 'Have a good day' when leaving for work.

Communication does not always happen at regular marker points in the day. This can leave me feeling disconnected and out of sync with Ben. Since he runs his own business, Ben is not restricted to any particular times of day for work. He often works into the small hours and wakes around lunchtime. He can get so focused on his work that he forgets to eat or go to the toilet. When I interrupt his focus to ask about dinner, his first response is often to run to the loo! He doesn't place the same importance on sharing rituals as I do but can carry them out if he is not too stressed or engrossed in work. If nothing is said at these times, I still receive a message. For example if he doesn't say good morning to me, he might be in pain. If I don't get a reply to my text he is probably deep in work and he won't be 'back' for some time.

Love for each other – e.g. 'I love you', 'I want to be with you' or 'Let's stay together.'

We found the 'Five Love Languages' online quiz really helpful. The concept breaks down how we naturally show our love to others and understand others' love for us into five distinct 'languages' or approaches. Confusion, hurt and misunderstanding can arise when people within a couple speak different 'love languages'. Ben shows and receives love through affirmation, touch and gifts. I am strong on service and quality time. I find it difficult to believe any words if there is no practical action to back them up! The challenge is to learn to accept love in all the forms it appears and to show it in ways that it will be understood – even if it's not our natural way! We both enjoy physical touch – especially hand-holding and hugs. They are simple and safe gestures that we can do most of the time.

Special interests – e.g. Incomprehensible equations and corresponding graphs!

Ben likes to talk to me about his special interest (also his business). I don't understand everything he says but I ask questions to help move the conversation forward. If he explained everything to me, he wouldn't get the help he is looking for as it would take me years to understand everything! Sometimes I get tired during these conversations and become less responsive – this usually happens late at night. However, Ben keeps talking because he says that, although he notices that I have gone quiet, I am kind enough to keep listening despite being tired. Eventually I tell him I am too tired to talk any more and that I'm going to bed and I take myself away!

Extras – chitchat, jokes, news, weather and gossip, e.g. 'This funny thing happened today...' or 'Did you hear what happened on the news?'

These are some of the 'non-essential' areas where we can run out of energy for communication. During stressful periods, communication that is important to me becomes non-essential for Ben. I look to neurotypical people around me to fill the gaps and I aim to connect with an NT every day.

Communication in our relationship is mostly intentional and usually tiring. We are two very different people sharing space and plans and love as best we can. Our relationship is so much smoother than it used to be, now that we know about AS and the differences between us are out in the open. There is less pretence, more honesty, and communication is clearer. We have learned so much so far, and I'm sure there are many more things for us to discover about ourselves and each other.

BEN'S STORY

Welcome to my AS wonderland. It's pretty much the same as the neurotypical (NT) world, with a few small changes here and there. First off, communication is still the same – sugar gets burned, information gets moved around.

Interpersonal communication is slightly different, but to understand the difference you'd need to be aware of synaesthesia. It's a strange neurological condition (more common amongst creative types) where the senses blur and overlap in atypical ways. For instance, for some synaesthetes, numbers have colours, for others shapes have smells, for others letters have personalities and some can taste words.

Curiously though, neurotypicals appear to have a synaesthesia between words and emotional response. For NTs, sentences have feelings. As do facial expressions. It appears that NTs have a profound experience of emotion in response to muscular contractions and sets of words.

This synaesthesia is sufficiently widespread that an AS person can learn to correlate facts about what NT people experience by studying their words and corresponding facial expressions. We can then start to try and simulate it and predict what things might be like for an NT person. As you can imagine, it's not a trivial task and requires quite some concentration, zapping your energy in the process. So, whilst one might become quite adept at it, it wouldn't become an ongoing process unless you were prepared to do nothing else.

As an AS person, I see the NT words/muscular-feelings synaesthesia as something of an impediment to efficient communication. You can see examples of NTs succeeding in military, technical and aviation communication by detaching words from emotion. Clear, unemotional communication is the most efficient.

In the widespread project to overcome this impediment to efficient communication, NTs have devised workarounds – using phraseology and posture to deliberately imply emotional content. This allows them to encode additional sub-textual information into their communication. Three examples are insinuation, sarcasm and flirting. An AS person paying attention can decode this but, again, it takes a lot of effort and is often secondary information anyway and so gets ignored.

In other words, I can work out what you mean – if I have the energy, time and brain space. If you'll excuse me, I'll just pop out the back, switch on the NT simulator and feed in whatever you just said. Stick the kettle on, I'll just be a minute...

Likewise, if I need to communicate something important, I can run it through the NT simulator in my head and check it doesn't contain any unintended emotional content. Again, it'll take some time.

The rest of the time, can we just pass information around – as a means of communicating – with no emotion attached? Us Aspies are working on making the world a better place and we have special interests with which we can do that. We might just be the next important evolutionary mutation for the human brain too. We don't have the time or energy to constantly decipher the emotions behind your words.

For instance, at work the other day, I needed to ask a colleague, Lisa, a technical question and, as part of my plan to be more sociable, I wandered over towards her office. The door was open and another colleague, Mark, was leaning against the doorframe. He was trying, with partial success, to relax as many of the muscles that were visible to Lisa as he could manage, but his legs and lower spine were a giveaway that he was tense. As I walked down the hallway, he leant backwards for a second, smiling and with his arms loose; most likely recoiling from a joke. The corners of his eyes showed progressive relaxation over the next second or two as he leant forwards again, his head disappearing past the doorframe. I notice things like this. 'He's flirting', I decipher, 'and she's not obviously rebuffing him'. In a previous meeting where Lisa had been sitting staring into space, his name had come up and she had flicked her eyes to another point and reddened very slightly. Again, you notice these things when you're AS and paying attention. 'So', I think, 'assuming he stays calm, he'll get a date out of it'. I decide to stand there for a minute and wait until he has finished asking her out. It seems the right thing to do.

As he walks away from me, his ears visibly rise a millimetre and he's grinning from ear to ear – so she said yes then. That means she should be in a good mood too. I walk up to the door, count to three, knock and go in. Her pupils are slightly dilated and she's straightening her back. That date should go well.

I ask Lisa my question, she answers, and her answer is going to create a lot more work for me. I say, 'Your design is bad and you should feel bad,' quoting an internet meme from *Futurama* and pondering how I'll rework my design to account for the changes that will be needed. And then it occurs to me that I've just spoken without content-checking my words. And now I'm not thinking about the work any more. Now I'm working out whether I have created a problem with the wrong words. Does she know that meme? Have we ever discussed *Futurama*? Does she even watch cartoons? She's in a good mood from Mark asking her out, but that could actually make her more vulnerable to emotional suggestion, and I've literally just told her to feel bad. OK, eyes back on her. Focus. What's her face doing? 'Um', I say, buying time for the previous chain of thoughts to empty out, so I can get back to figuring out what just happened. She's not making eye contact, that rules out anything massively extreme. Sides of eyes are relaxed, lips pursed; she's about to say something. 'The...design... was in your heart, not in your hands?' she says, quoting the line before the meme from the *Futurama* episode. I'm saved. It's fine. It'll be OK. I haven't caused an incident. I think I need a cup of tea now. I should smile. I do a smile and relax my shoulders best I can. No idea what they were doing during that little incident, but I felt them move, so that's not great. Probably she didn't notice if she wasn't looking at my face. Oh, there's a double meaning in using that quote 'design...not in your hands'. She's telling me it's her design not mine. Right.

'Understood; I'll get to work on it' I say and duck out of her office as fast as I can without looking weird. I am going to just concentrate on walking back to my desk and sitting down for a bit.

Tony Attwood's Commentary and Q&A

This is a chapter where I'd really like to commend Alice for her descriptions. They are so eloquent and insightful, especially the first, about wrapping a present. *'I can take offence at the way his communication is wrapped... I am learning to look for the underlying message rather than get distracted by the unusual delivery.'* This is about the AS partner not seeing the need for sugar-coating anything, being the self-appointed revealer of the truth: this is the truth, why should I worry about your feelings?

Now, the next section is, in part, on sensory sensitivity and this is worth exploring here. The sensory sensitivity is very real and incredibly painful for the AS partner, and their quick response can be one of anger and agitation. This can be very confusing to the NT partner who won't necessarily understand the severe reaction to a sensory experience, which might seem fairly innocuous to them. But it is incredibly painful for the person with AS, whose immediate and instinctive reaction is a fight-or-flight response, and that can be a real problem. There needs to be an understanding of what those triggers and circumstances are.

An interesting revelation here: *'I am starting to notice a link between Ben coming across to me as rude and his anxiety levels.'* From my point of view as a clinician, the depth of anxiety influences the depth of AS. Some Asperger behaviours that are components of the diagnostic criteria – routines and rituals for example – are actually behavioural mechanisms for coping with anxiety. So yes, the more anxious the person is the more socially withdrawn they will be, the more rigid in thinking, the more engaged in the special interest. So anxiety will definitely influence the level of expression of AS.

What Alice is doing is using symbols for communication. For example, red might be 'I don't understand, please explain again' or 'I can't think of a reply'. Again, this may seem somewhat artificial but it may be a necessary way to improve clarity in communication between partners. At times of emotion the person with AS may not be able to articulate their feelings, but if they have a pre-prepared card to explain it, they can just choose the card and pass it to their NT partner, and this allows the partner to focus on the text and not on the intensity of the emotion. I think this is a great idea and I would encourage other couples to use the same approach that Alice and Ben have, which is, more or less, a translation of thoughts and feelings in particular situations. It helps enormously if they're written down in advance.

> *I've been learning to make my statements in a bold way so that they are noticed and get more of a response. It feels similar to writing a birthday card to a child who is learning to read. We make our letters larger and clearer so they are recognized. It can feel a little exaggerated but it is more appropriate for the purpose.*

I would like to thank Alice again for giving a wonderful description and her metaphors are brilliant. You have to speak in a way your AS partner will understand and that means you have to be very clear.

'*Some of the things Ben says feel empty, fake and distant. They leave me feeling more alone than no response at all.*' Yes, that's the risk, that sometimes, although your AS partner may give you the response that you want, you feel you know it's contrived and what you are seeking is something intuitive and real. It can feel as though these are just vacuous words. But which would you prefer – nothing, or the right words but they seem vacuous? That's a decision you have to make yourself.

'*[He] is really good at making people feel included in social situations even though he finds it exhausting.*' Yes, and for the NT partner, that's part of the Cassandra syndrome. Other people see this person being social and seemingly adept in social situations but do not see what the NT partner experiences, that behind closed doors, the impact of that effort for the AS partner is absolute exhaustion and a need to be alone, sometimes for hours, in order to recover.

'*I came up with the following categories.*' There are eight categories, and I think Alice is a natural psychologist. I don't know what her career is, but she is very intuitive in this area and I wholeheartedly endorse her descriptions.

I find Ben's story illuminating too.

Curiously though, neurotypicals appear to have a synaesthesia between words and emotional response. For NTs, sentences have feelings. As do facial expressions. It appears that NTs have a profound experience of emotion in response to muscular contractions and sets of words.

He's making a very intellectual observation of people.

...an AS person can learn to correlate facts about what NT people experience by studying their words and corresponding facial expressions. We can then start to try and simulate it and predict what things might be like for an NT person. As you can imagine, it's not a trivial task and requires some concentration, zapping your energy in the process.

Wow! So this is a genius intellect trying to understand basic social emotional behaviour. It makes no sense to them because it's not based on logic but emotion. The Aspie quality is in logic, not in emotion, and Ben is intellectually trying to predict people by their emotions and reading all their signals.

He says here that *'[c]lear, unemotional communication is the most efficient'*. Yes it is – but NTs don't do that all the time. He says he can work out what NTs mean if he has *'the energy, time and brain space. Stick the kettle on. I'll just be a minute...'* That's processing time. In other words it's a big problem for the human computer, the brain. Rather than giving a spontaneous answer, for the Aspie, it requires some thought. A person with AS will need time to process before responding to situations. This is different to most NT partners who have the ability to be intuitive and respond accordingly, often spontaneously, to situations. For the AS partner, having that processing time is vital and increases their chances of giving the 'right' response. If the AS individual is sitting staring blankly rather than responding immediately to something you've asked, it is likely to be due to this need to process. In other words 'I haven't got enough information, I can't compute, I need more data before I can respond.'

Why is shouting and irritability often the packaging that people with AS use to communicate?
Because they don't know how to be subtle, there are only intense emotions. So, when any emotion is attached to what they do, it's at maximum volume.

How important is it for the NT partner to learn to read the message behind the AS partner's action?
It is vital. But it's a two-way process, and sometimes the AS partner may be making a judgement on insufficient information. Then, when they get it wrong, they can become emotional and have an explosion.

Why are visual forms of communication, such as the traffic light card system that Alice mentioned, so helpful?
Because it puts information down in written form, which is a better way of explaining to someone with AS, what's going on. I know it's contrived and artificial but it works, and sometimes you need that. Because otherwise the alternative is a row and everyone's hurt. It's basically row prevention.

Alice talks about changing communication style. How far should both partners compromise on how they do things?
The reality is that it is not always going to be 50/50. It's more likely to be 70/30 (in favour of the NT partner doing the majority of compromising) and sometimes more like 90/10.

Why do people with Asperger's withdraw? Is it important to understand the reasons behind this and to find ways of reducing those times?
Well, they withdraw because it's the cure for AS. All the diagnostic criteria of AS disappear in solitude. You can't have a social emotional reciprocity problem if you're alone. You can't have a problem reading body language if you're alone, and you can't have a problem maintaining relationships if you're alone. You can have your routines and rituals that soothe and calm you without disrupting the activities of other people. When you're alone, your sensory sensitivity is minimized. You can have your special interest as long as you like because you can't be stopped by an NT partner who doesn't understand it. So the cure is solitude: when you're in a room on your own, you're cured. The moment somebody comes in or you walk out, that's when you have AS. Also, the level of stress and AS is proportional to the number of people present. Two's company, three's a crowd. For someone with AS, solitude is their emotional restorative – an enjoyable experience – and can also be their processing time. So withdrawal has many functions: cure, processing time, emotional restoration and enjoyment. So Aspies

NEURODIVERSE RELATIONSHIPS

need it. The problem is, if you're running a family, it's very hard to find time alone.

What are your top tips for effective communication in an AS relationship?
I've made a list of the things I would recommend for better communication. This is not necessarily in order of priority:

- Say what you mean and mean what you say. Be clear, unambiguous and direct. It's almost like creating – within your speech – a highlighter pen indicating 'this is important'.

- Learn to understand how they communicate and the need for processing time. Understand that they will want to correct errors. And that a conversation to them is all about an exchange of information. Be aware that, to someone with AS, idioms and figures of speech can be confusing.

- Finally, understand that communication by any other means may be better than talking. Alice's description of the traffic light system and cards that she and Ben use is a good example of this. Find different ways to explain and communicate; maybe find a clip from a movie, a music track or a google image to illustrate what it is you're trying to convey.

In other words, the problem within communication for a person with Asperger's syndrome is when it is face-to-face speech. Most would prefer anything other than 'look at me' and 'tell me'.

4

Diagnosis

TOM'S STORY

I guess there is no real beginning to this story, unless to take my birth as a start. But I'm not going to bore you that much. Let's just say that, for as long as I can remember, people have driven me to distraction and that my 'nobody understands me' teenage phase has gone on a bit too long.

So let's begin with my wife, Liz, as she plays an integral part in this story.

We met ten years ago via an internet dating site. I'm not now, or ever was, able to go out to bars and talk to women – or anybody really.

I digress. We got together and got on brilliantly. Liz is beautiful, funny and smart. She is very clever and knows how to use her intelligence. To me, she was a breath of fresh air. You see, the gods of fate decided to have a bit of fun with me: my wife is a psychologist. When we met she wasn't practising, she was working in an off-licence. She, like me, likes to take the scenic route! As with most relationships, at the start there were ups and downs while we got to know each other, but we stuck with it.

After a few years we had our son and we kept on going... but things weren't quite right. We argued, or rather *she* argued. I said nothing or very little. She talked, I listened; but I didn't really understand what she was saying. Oh, I nodded in the right places but what I heard when she was trying to explain to me what I'd done was, 'Fghoreg oeghbkjadgnj sgfnjk fhjkff'. I understood the words she was saying, but not in the context of *me*. Why did she find this particular thing so annoying? What was it I had said that was so wrong?

One night we were in the kitchen when she stopped me and said, 'I think a penny has just dropped.' The rest of the conversation went something like this...

'Oh, er, OK ... hmmm, what?'

'I think you might have Asperger's.'

'A burger's what?'

'It's a form of autism that would explain some of the things I've noticed.'

'Oh... OK... well we can look into it...'

And that's the way it was left for a few years. Life, once again, took over and I tried to fit in and do whatever I could to make my wife and son happy. It didn't work...

The job I was in at the time wasn't a healthy place for me to be, so I started to withdraw into myself, talking less and less. I had to get away from it.

We had planned to move to the area my wife was from, mostly so that my son could go to a good school but also because of its rural location. I'm quite an outdoor person, so the pull was there. In the meantime, though, Liz had returned to her profession and, while we were both in jobs that we didn't want to be in, we just got on with it. However, as luck would have it, Liz got a job back home. We moved and, fortunately, I got a job... in IT of course!

Things moved along nicely. We moved and got settled in, yet I still had an itch I couldn't scratch. Meanwhile, Liz couldn't quite get to grips with my moods, silence or lack of, well, normality.

As she was now working with people like me, more pennies began to drop. My unerring sense of direction (just had to get that in there); my noticing the smallest detail while missing the big picture; knowing stuff that isn't really much use except in a pub quiz. The list goes on.

'I have a test here', my wife said one day. 'Would you like to do it?'

'OK', I replied, 'what is it?'

'It's the Autism Quotient (AQ) test.'

'Er right. Hmm, what's it for?'

'Well, I need to practise it', my wife continued, 'and also it might answer a lot of questions for you'.

So we did it. We spent an evening going through the test and she spent longer scoring it. And the result? Well, I'm here now, writing this...

Has knowing about my Asperger's syndrome made a difference to my life? Yes and no. It hasn't changed who I am or what I do, but it has given me a better understanding of why I do what I do.

People still bug me just as much and I still need to hide from the world (people) every once in a while. But, with understanding comes power. Power over who and what I am and of my future. It also brings a sense of wonder. I see it when my wife talks about others like me – the wonder of seeing things differently, the wonder of exploration. I never was one to take the easy or short route, there's no fun in that...

An NT Perspective

LIZ'S STORY

I met my husband, Tom, in the summer of 2005. We exchanged a few emails after initially connecting on an online dating site, met up a few times, and it progressed from there.

Our story of increasing awareness, 'diagnosis' and, ultimately, recognition and acceptance by both of us started way back then, although I didn't know it. There were always some slightly strange incongruities that didn't seem to quite fit with the kind, principled and intelligent man I was getting to know. Having noted them, but not having any framework to make sense of them at the time, I simply 'parked' them and moved on. These were all the things that, later, were to fall into place at once – like many pennies dropping. For example: the relentlessness and honesty with which I was pursued – no game-playing here; the fact that he seemed to have retained a modicum of Canadian accent after returning from a two-week holiday there; the fact that he pretty much sat and stared at me for the duration of our first restaurant date! More disconcerting, however, were the tasteless remarks made about the London bombings, which occurred within the first few months of us meeting. Having reflected on this many times since, I think this was a particularly telling incident, coming as it did during the early stages of courtship, at a time he was actively trying to impress! Then there was his arrogance, his peculiar relationship with food and his phenomenal ability to absorb random facts (and spew them back at people as if he'd known them for years and they were stupid not to have known!). I remember clearly one pivotal moment, again early on, when I had resolved to end the relationship because we did not think the same way. Telling him this, however, resulted in an impassioned, logical but rather forceful argument about all the ways he thought we did think in the same way – and therefore should stay together. I was persuaded. I stayed.

A trained clinical psychologist, I was having some time out of the profession at the time we met, but a few years later (after the birth of our son in 2007) I returned to the job. Previously in adult mental health, this time I would be working with children in a Child and Adolescent Mental Health Service (CAMHS). A lot of children and young people came through the doors and often our job was to act as kind of detectives, working out which factors (biological, environmental or psychological) might have led to them or their family presenting with a particular set of difficulties. Quite often we were the first professionals to identify the possibility of an autistic spectrum condition or other neurodevelopmental condition in a young person. Our job was to gather relevant information before referring them on to a specialist diagnostic service. Still it did not occur to me that my husband might also be on the spectrum.

At home, our relationship was largely going well, but I was continuing to encounter anomalies that I was trying to make sense of. The area of touch and intimacy was an early casualty. It had become apparent that Tom did not know his own strength and failed also to respond to the usual subtle signs to stop or let go of, for example, a hug. As a result, I would end up tense and defensive during any intimate moments, not knowing when the next accidental hurt was coming. I recall many, many attempts (face-to-face initially and, when this didn't work, by text or email) in which I tried, using all I knew about appropriate assertiveness and communication, to give him feedback and help him learn about my preferences. I remember at one point in my pregnancy he refused to have sex with me any more because I 'didn't smell right'! However, for the most part, it was he who was interested and I who was not. Strictly speaking, I was, but could not get my body to respond in the absence of responsive, intuitive touch and emotional closeness. I remember the following years being particularly difficult as the conversations about our intimate life got more and more fraught and emotional. I remember questioning my sanity. I tried separating out my own issues. 'Maybe I'm just hypersensitive to touch,' I thought. 'Maybe it's a result of the pain of childbirth or that old sports injury?' But I still realized that there was something odd about Tom's response. 'Is it some kind of attachment or trauma response?' I wondered. 'Is he stuck at the emotional and physical level of a 14-year-old because of his experiences? Is there some big trauma he isn't telling me about?' This turned out not to be the case.

Meanwhile, in my work environment, I recall attending a training event on autism in older adolescents and young adults, run by an educational psychologist. This was my turning point. I remember the moment all the pennies dropped at once. Strangely, it wasn't when an obvious piece of information about autism was highlighted – it was in response to a (possibly throwaway) comment about how people on the spectrum, despite having strong opinions, would not be good debaters (because of their cognitive inflexibility). Suddenly I understood why everything that was taught to us that day about how to relate to someone on the spectrum felt like common sense. I had been doing it for about four years! I remember mentioning tentatively to my (psychologist) boss at the time that I thought my husband might be on the spectrum. She laughed. I remember saying, 'No, really'. I must have bought a few books and recognized bits of Tom all the way through.

I have a very clear memory of the first conversation I had with him about the subject. I'd told him I wanted to talk about something and remember thinking, as I entered the room, book in hand, and saw him huddled up inside the hood of his cardigan, his arms folded defensively across his chest, that he looked freakily reminiscent of some of the young, male, autistic youths I was seeing in the clinic. I presented him with the book, I read aloud examples and made the argument that this sounded very like him. At that time his response was non-committal. He suggested maybe I was afflicted with 'medical student syndrome', where you start to see examples everywhere of the particular condition you are studying! Recently though, he told me he knew I was on to something from the very start.

Following this, I spent the next couple of years holding the theory that Tom might be autistic as a possibility. There was still doubt in my mind. Our battle to connect on an intimate level continued. We tried two different relationship therapists. The first time, my very tentative suggestion that my husband might have Asperger's was quickly dismissed. The second time, put more assertively, it was not dismissed but I was asked, rather clumsily, how I felt, 'now that I had put my husband in a box'. I was not happy and said so, and no amount of backtracking by the counsellor was going to win my trust. Also, in each of these situations I watched my poor husband – very much not a talker but committed to the process for the sake of the relationship – squirm. It was destructive to both of us.

Somewhere in this period was the moment I moved from 'maybe' to 'definitely' in my head. We'd had a lovely evening-in together, the fire was lit and the lights were low. I was sitting on the floor at his knees, feeling somewhat in the mood for romance. I was practically rubbing my head against his legs. 'Right!' he exclaimed suddenly, getting up, 'Tea and toast then!' I was frustrated. I was furious. However, his response to me was that of complete surprise. He said he had no idea of my intentions. Again, the sound of pennies dropping.

For me, at a really deep level, that was my moment of diagnosis. I kept 'bumping into' his autism over and over again in so many subtle ways. Yet, from the outside looking in, I could see that it was not obvious. He 'passed' well; he had friends, he could say the right things. He enjoyed his mountain biking, yes, but was he any more obsessive than any other mountain biker? 'I think you're too subtle', I would say to him, 'to be picked up by any diagnostic service. I only see it because I live with you. You're too motivated not to be caught out. Anyway, you don't have the obsessive part.'

Sometime around then at work, having relocated and started in a new job back in adult mental health, I had established that there was no formal local pathway or service for the diagnosis of adults with autism. Fascinated by the whole area, I had muscled myself onto a subgroup responsible for developing just such a service. I was in the fortunate position to be able to take up the offer of training in the Adult Asperger's Assessment (AAA) in Cambridge. This approach uses the Autism Quotient (AQ), Empathy Quotient (EQ) and Relatives Questionnaire (RQ) as screening tools. As always, I used my ever-willing husband as a guinea pig for the questionnaires. He filled them in, dismissive as ever, stating that they weren't that great, that he could see what answers they were looking for, and that he was sure he'd filled them in just the same way as anyone else. The scores shocked both of us. His AQ was 35

(80% of those scoring 32 or more have a diagnosis of AS), his EQ was 16 (80% of those scoring 30 or less have a diagnosis of AS). My 'mildly autistic' husband was not so mild at all!

Soon after, we watched a documentary about autism. In it, an Asperger's couple was interviewed. They talked about being each other's 'spoonful' of social contact. Also shown was a psychological experiment with autistic and non-autistic children. The experimenter showed children a box with a reward in it (a toy or sweet) and demonstrated tapping on its lid before opening it. The neurotypical children played along with this 'game' with obvious enjoyment, taking their lead from the experimenter. The autistic children just opened the box. You could almost hear them thinking, 'Just open the box, for ****'s sake, are you mad?' This completely typifies Tom's approach to the world – and I think he recognized it too. These were the two events which brought him fully on board in accepting his 'diagnosis'.

Knowing about Tom's Asperger's has helped us a lot, I think. It has certainly helped me and I think it has helped him to understand himself. We occasionally have 'deep and meaningfuls' about it after a few glasses of wine on a weekend night, as that is the only time Tom will ever really let his guard down. He's said many poignant things such as, in relation to his phenomenal defensiveness, 'I don't see into other people, so I don't know how much into me they can see.' Or the classic 'You and that rock out there are the same to me – I only know you have feelings because you tell me you do.' And, recently, in response to my gentle ribbing at how frustrated he was getting with the 'stupid' behaviour of the lead characters in a zombie film, walking to their death, 'How can I put it? Those people... they're as real to me as you are!'

He hasn't really told many people about his AS as he doesn't feel it would help his cause much at work (as an IT professional), but he's generously told me that he has no objections to my sharing it with people I might want to talk to. We have, on the odd occasion, discussed whether or not we can, or even need, to make his diagnosis 'official'. We keep talking about getting round to me filling in the formal AAA interview schedule and documenting all the evidence for each section. It's there – even the 'obsessional' bits are starting to show now we own our own house and it is ours to do with what we will! However, I'm not sure that a diagnosis by your wife would ever be truly accepted – no matter how well documented!

I am now officially a diagnostician myself and also work therapeutically with adults who have both autism and mental health problems. When I feel on an even keel myself, being surrounded by such courageous, engaging, creative and unusual individuals is energizing and a total privilege. When I am not, and I need to be taken care of emotionally, it is a desperate place to be. I need my neurotypical friends. It's just as well that when it comes to the analogy of the 'cactus' (autistic individuals) and the 'rose' (neurotypicals), I am more of a spider plant. I can go a long time without watering. I may eventually wilt without it, but I recover quickly.

Tony Attwood's Commentary and Q&A

In this chapter, Liz talks about *'the relentlessness and honesty with which I was pursued'*. The romantic pursuit from a person with AS can be very intoxicating but it doesn't last. It has its use-by-date.

The other interesting thing to note is that Liz trained as a clinical psychologist. We often find that the partner of a person with Asperger's is either a fellow Aspie (they're both engineers or accountants) or they work in the caring profession (psychology, nursing, teaching, etc.). So it's someone who is naturally talented in understanding the perspective of others, who can get into the mind-set of the Aspie. That's what's appealing to the person with AS. To the Aspie, this is the first person ever to understand them. The problem is, you may understand some of him, but not all of him.

Liz describes the area of touch and intimacy as a *'casualty'*. They didn't have sex anymore because she *'didn't smell right'*. This is an illustration of the sensory sensitivity of the person with AS. Liz goes on to say that she *'could not get my body to respond in the absence of responsive, intuitive touch and emotional closeness'*. The lack of closeness, touch and intimacy is going to be a major contributor to depression in the neurotypical partner. There is, from my clinical experience, a major risk of depression in the neurotypical partner, both as a reaction to missing out on the things that act as an antidote to depression and also living with circumstances that create a feeling of depression.

From Tom's point of view he says, *'I don't see into other people, so I don't know how much into me they can see.'* It's the classic analogy of *'You and that rock out there are the same to me – I only know you have feelings because you tell me you do.'* So if they can't read the signals, if they don't read emotions, then they don't know what emotions are going on within you.

I also like the analogy to the cactus and the rose and Liz likening herself to a spider plant: *'I can go a long time without watering. I may eventually wilt... but I recover quickly'.* That's a good metaphor.

What would you say to neurotypicals who often struggle with their AS partner's tasteless, insensitive or what seem downright rude remarks?
It's not rudeness in the sense that they've been badly brought up or that they're not a nice person. It's more a question of being oblivious to how the true comment will affect the feelings of other people. Being self-appointed 'revealers of the truth', they will say what comes into their mind without previously mentally scanning it or proofreading it for how other people will feel or how they will receive it. There is no consideration of a Plan B – of another way of getting the message across in a more palatable way. It's not nasty or rude, and the AS person can become quite upset when challenged because it wasn't their intention to upset anyone. It's quite a revelation to them when you try and explain 'It's not necessarily *what* you said, it's the *way* you said it'. But people with Asperger's syndrome do not hear themselves as other people do. I think, mentally, they're going through the information and conveying it, but they don't consider emotion in the way they say those words in order to make them more acceptable for the other person. That can be really challenging for them.

It seems that often, both the person on the spectrum and the neurotypical partner can't quite put their finger on what is different, only that there is a sense of being different. How common is this sense of difference for those with Asperger's syndrome in your experience?
It's very common. In the diagnostic assessment I often ask, 'When did you first notice you were different?' For some it was pre-school, for others it is between the ages of six and eight years old. That's when they start to know they're different, and the responses are either escaping into imagination, imitating, becoming arrogant or getting depressed. Those are the four most common reactions to that feeling of being different, and it's possible for all four to occur at different times.

Is not knowing their own physical strength a part of AS?
It's another way of not being aware of how their actions may be affecting other people. For neurotypicals, this realization acts as the stop sign. But if you can't read people, you can't see the red light to stop.

Liz describes how frustrated Tom gets with characters behaving stupidly in a film. Is it common for people with AS not to differentiate between fiction and reality?

I talked about one of the ways of coping being to escape into imagination and fiction, to a world where they belong and they feel successful. For example, an AS person may write fiction or make movies, and that becomes so intoxicating and enjoyable that they almost want to inhabit a make-believe world, sometimes even having imaginary friends or pets. But then they become so engrossed in it they may start to have difficulty in determining the difference between reality and fiction. They may not understand how other people are confused by the way they are almost living out their fiction. They might even say, 'I want to be called by a different name.'

Is social media a hero or a villain for people with autism?

Social media has many components. Sometimes it becomes a social connection in terms of playing games online where they don't have to socialize traditionally. They play the game and they're valued in that game because they're practised at it, they're a master. So, in this sense, social media can be a great confidence booster for the Aspie. For the first time, people want to know them and be associated with them because they're good at the game. So it bolsters self-esteem and it can provide a social connection. The problem is that social media can also become addictive, which can be especially detrimental within a relationship when much more time is spent on the computer than with the family and face-to-face relationships. So, in answer to the question, it can be both.

Why do people with autism tend to notice the smallest detail while missing the big picture?

This is what psychologists call weak central coherence, which is a common characteristic of AS. It's a part of the cognitive profile – paying great attention to detail. If you change the detail, you've changed the whole picture but being over-focused on the detail, there is no understanding of the big picture – the gist of what's going on. For example, if studying history at school, having to learn and recall dates will come easily. However, being asked to comment on something like the gestalt of the origins of the Second World War is probably going to be much more challenging because making it coherent and not getting side-tracked is going to be a problem.

Tom talks about the wonder of seeing things differently, the wonder of exploration. How can Asperger's be seen in a positive light? What benefits can we take from it?

Asperger's syndrome provides a different way of perceiving, thinking, learning and relating. Sometimes it's important not to make a value judgement that the AS way of thinking is inferior in some way. It's just different. In societal terms this different way of thinking can lead to great advances in science and the arts. A person with Asperger's can be very good in crises. But, if you're in a close, personal relationship with that person, it can be a problem. I describe it as a bit like fire: society needs fire for warmth and light and cooking, but if you're too close to it, it can burn.

5

Empathy

This chapter is dedicated to Victor John Burgess
(12 May 1959 – 11 June 2017)

An NT Perspective

SANDRA'S STORY

Like anyone, I suffer from stress at times, and this affects my ability to communicate with my husband in a calm way. When I get stressed, Victor's quite a good person to have around as he doesn't react like I do to the things that wind me up. Often he'll smile or laugh if it's not a serious incident that's set me off, and this frequently makes me stop and look at how unreasonable my reactions are. His calmness helps me to take a look at my own behaviour and often I end up laughing too. In that sense Victor's a really good listener, allowing me to let off steam about things that don't directly concern *him*.

However, when I'm upset by *his* behaviour specifically, things between us can quickly go from bad to worse. I end up yelling or crying and Victor withdraws further into himself. We've had so many times like this where I've been very angry and cannot get Victor to understand why I'm so upset. It often results in me refusing to talk to him, ignoring him as a way to make him feel bad (which doesn't help at all, and I'm not proud of behaving that way). Through it all, I still hope that he'll figure it out by himself, but this very rarely happens. I can think of one particular time when I'd pretty much stopped communicating with him and was feeling hopeless and depressed about our relationship; we were in the car, and he suddenly pulled over into a lay-by and asked me what was wrong. I think that's the only time this has ever happened! I was so grateful for that, it really helped. Because the problem with Vic's difficulty in empathizing is that, as a consequence, I very often feel quite alone, like I'm the 'adult' partner who has to explain everything regarding our emotional life together. That can be really hard at times.

But as the years have gone on (we've been together for eight years now), and the more I understand Victor as a person, the better I'm getting at organizing my life so that I don't get caught up in feeling emotionally *different* or *wrong*. This can happen if the

83

non-AS partner gets locked into the kind of life their AS partner would seemingly prefer. That's what I've found the long-term path of an AS/NT pairing can often become – one where the neurotypical partner becomes isolated from their social set. I've tried hard not to let that happen. I fully accept it's Vic's choice not to interact with many other people apart from me. I don't mind that as long as I'm clear that it's my responsibility to stay connected to friends with a more recognizable kind of empathy. I mean my own friends, who I don't have to explain things to about how I feel. This keeps me mentally healthy. Basically, if I didn't have my own friends, who have nothing to do with my married life, I'd probably be unable to stay sane or married – or both!

Victor was brilliant when my mum died. We hadn't known each other for very long then, maybe six or eight months. Because he is so responsible, he drove up to my sister's house (45 miles away) to pick me up after we'd been to the hospital. He was very gentle with me, holding me while I sobbed. Later, when I came out of hospital after a hip replacement operation he looked after me really well, cooking (not very imaginatively, but, hey, I was grateful!) and even agreeing to give me the necessary course of injections in my stomach for what seemed like weeks afterwards. So I did feel looked after. I think practically, Victor can 'do' empathy when he knows what needs to be done. But, on the other hand, when he came to collect me from hospital another time, he was already very stressed because he'd had a hard time finding a parking space and made a big fuss because I had to ask him to go back up to the ward to collect shoes I'd forgotten. I was in a wheelchair at the hospital entrance. He could not understand why him being bad tempered and making a big deal out of having to go back to the ward upset me. I'd had a big operation three days previously – and he was angry that he had had to go back and collect my shoes!

There are many issues we've fallen out over which have never really been resolved, and this is difficult. I have tactics when we have to talk about serious issues. I make sure I am very calm, speak in a reasonable tone and don't start shouting when I feel myself getting exasperated with Victor's lack of input. If I even sniff in an angry tone of voice, he'll withdraw. Sometimes I can't be calm and I start shouting. When this happens, I try and remove myself from the confrontation rather than stay and make things worse. Generally, Vic will apologize if he understands what has happened and why it was making me upset. But the apology, when it comes, is always quite a while after the argument, hours or even a day later. I don't know, but suspect that this happens because Victor is processing what happened and figuring it out. When Vic doesn't apologize at all, things remain frosty on my side until they eventually just resume as normal. I find it too emotionally exhausting to stay angry. But of course this doesn't resolve the problem. I think I've accepted that we won't always be able to work things out. It's like there's a big blank in Victor's ability to understand when he has done or said something I've found offensive or emotionally cruel. I suppose because I know, in all our time together, he hasn't really learned to be more emotionally aware of how I am as a person, part of me can accept that he never will. I do understand that this is difficult for him. But it's tricky to remember this all the time, and also I don't want to treat him like he's so different that I have to act like I'm someone else.

I've tried asking Vic how he'd describe me. He always says, 'You're funny, and you're kind-hearted, and you're small.' Like that was a quality of my personality. I think that's when I realize that we are, to some extent, always going to be strangers to each other to some degree. But it doesn't make me sad. I like the fact that I'll never really know him fully. It keeps me interested. Is that odd? We have a good, sexually intimate relationship which is loving and real. We feel very close to each other that way. I think it's the one time when we are truly together.

I know Victor loves me. He knows I love him. We will get by, working out how to negotiate our difficulties and differences as we go. I was convinced Vic had Asperger's long before we got married, although he wasn't diagnosed until much later. But I need to point out something I believe is crucial: if Victor and I had had children together, I honestly don't think our marriage would have survived. I would have found the emotional loneliness, along with the additional responsibility, too much to bear without the diagnosis and without the emotional maturity I now have. Victor loves his children very much, but he does have a hard time empathizing with them and their lives. It has caused a rift in the family communication, but now the children know about his AS (they were told a year ago) I can only hope things will improve with time and their understanding.

After we'd lived together for about three years and I had recognized Vic was different but didn't have a huge amount of knowledge about AS, we went for counselling at Relate. It was of no use to us whatsoever. We had many problems with seeing Vic's children, which culminated in him going to 'Families Need Fathers', as I found it was too much for me to deal with as his only close friend. I suggested he should go as I was constantly overwhelmed with panic about the situation, being unable to intervene on his behalf, but wanting to defend him. Really I wanted him to sort it out himself, but he was simply unable to do this. He couldn't see that how he was being treated was abusive and I had to watch it affecting him, his children and their relationships. It was a very black time for all of us. As he wasn't diagnosed until January 2015, I felt lost in a muddle of messy emotions coming at me from all sides. The children were angry he'd left home, his ex-wife was angry and Vic was depressed trying to keep himself together with all this rage being fired at him, so I had to make a decision to stay or go and (obviously!) I decided to stay.

The hardest thing about that time was trying to understand what Vic was feeling, as he always plays things down and never got angry when he had a perfect right to be mad. I did a lot of coaxing to get Vic to talk about how upset he was when he seemed very sad. Then he would get mad at the wrong things – like having a massive fit while driving at someone driving in front of him doing something he thought was terrible, when it seemed quite innocent to me. I eventually figured out that these fits of anger (and they could be quite intense) while driving, were connected to text messages from his ex-wife that he hadn't shared with me. They were often really cruel, abusive and manipulative. I don't know why he didn't tell me about them but eventually he started sharing when he'd had a nasty text and this helped me understand his moods a bit better. Victor finds talking about anything emotional very difficult. Often his reactions are odd when he's upset, like shouting at other drivers when most people wouldn't be upset by what they were doing. Victor doesn't seem to recognize when he is getting stressed or upset. Whereas I'll say 'I'm getting upset now' or 'That wasn't a very nice thing to do' or 'What you said about so and so upset me and I feel...'. Victor doesn't verbalize his emotions. I am always telling him that I can't guess what's wrong, that it's too exhausting, and when I feel myself going into that guessing game, I stop. It took me a long time to learn to do that.

Now, as I'm writing, I'm wondering how we actually do communicate! I believe Victor does know when I'm upset and, because he trusts me to be honest and open with him, he will tell me what the problem is when he's upset – if and when *he* has figured it out! He needs time to work out why he feels bad, generally. I know that about him and it's OK. I suppose then, we've come quite a long way in our particular kind of empathizing as a couple. Victor can now apologize if he knows he has upset me – and my having to explain why I am upset has become second nature. I don't think that's a bad thing. I think it's positive that Victor has helped me to become more honest and vocal in having to spell out my emotional reactions to events. I like the fact that we don't 'play games'. I still fall into my old, familiar ways of being sometimes and will yell and want to make him feel bad; but those times are rare, thankfully, and usually we can avoid them. We share the same sense of humour and we both love books and nature. Laughter often saves us from arguments. He will always make me laugh. I think he's a wonderful man.

An AS Perspective

VICTOR'S STORY

Although I was not finally diagnosed with Asperger's syndrome (AS) until January 2015, after a long wait to get a diagnosis, I have always known that I was 'different' in some ways from most other people. I have lived with this all my life, as early as I can remember from my school days. I know this has held me back in many ways during my life – at work, with my career and also in my relationships.

Ironically, I spent the early part of my working life in the specialization of communications, serving with the Royal Navy. It was even commented on at one point by a shipmate that 'for somebody working in communications, you aren't a very good communicator'. Fair comment!

My earliest memory of being different or finding life difficult is on the garden swing as a child. I would swing furiously to relieve my frustrations. I still have photographs of me doing this, with a scowl on my face! When I was a little older, at secondary school, I would come home from school and beat up my teddy bear to take out my frustrations from the day's events.

In earlier years I used to think that I was just shy and awkward. But I'm not really sure that 'shy' is the right description. Somewhere along the way I seem to have missed out on learning the niceties of 'normal' social communication. I led quite a sheltered upbringing as my sister was a lot older than me and had left home by the time I started school. My parents did not have a car and didn't do very much socializing either, so I spent a lot of time left to my own devices. I was always well cared for and knew that I was very much loved and wanted. My parents' story had been interrupted by World War Two, and, despite first meeting in their teens, by the time I was born, they were in their early forties and, I'm sure, affected by their experiences of the war. My father was a Japanese prisoner of war and spent several years badly treated out in Burma. My mother was quite unwell during her pregnancy, and I know that there was a chance that either my mother or I might not

88

have survived. I think this resulted in us being quite a close-knit family. If anything, I may have been over-protected by my parents. However, I was certainly allowed to go out and away from the home when I was a little older and did not feel mollycoddled at all.

Although 'somewhat of a loner' (a phrase I recall was used by one of the Royal Navy divisional officers writing up my report) I am not completely averse to company and do always seek out a kindred soul of some sort to keep me company. I eventually saw this as me being more selective than most about who I associate with and have been quite the opposite of the easily-led 'sheep' types who will go along with anything just to fit in with the crowd.

I know that I am averse to any kind of conflict and will always shy away from a confrontation unless absolutely necessary. This certainly caused problems in many of my relationships and was a factor in the failure of my first marriage. The more my ex-wife would try to goad me into some kind of reaction or response, the more I would retreat into my shell and not come out until the storm had blown over! Obviously, this is very detrimental in the long term, as issues do not get resolved and lie dormant and simmering, ultimately creating long-term resentment.

Despite this, I do have a strong sense of right and wrong and will not stray from my principles. I am also very loyal.

I feel that Sandra and I are much better now at talking things through openly and honestly and, whilst this doesn't mean we never fall out, it makes life a lot easier and more successful. When we do argue, I know I am not often very good at apologizing and can't explain why this is. I know that I am not above acknowledging when I am in the wrong and, if anything, probably feel in the wrong more often than not!

I know that my children have found life difficult with me and their mother not always getting on 'normally', and I believe that they do understand deep down that I love them and care very much about them. I know that they have sometimes felt that I don't care about them in the way they might expect me to. I found some aspects of being a father quite difficult, although I was quite happy to engage in the day-to-day chores of childcare such as nappy changes, feeding, reading stories, playing, etc. I did find it quite hard to entertain two pre-school children whilst their mother was trying to sleep after her night shifts. I would often end up taking the children out and trying to find places to entertain them – though my ideas of entertainment were more of the country and beach-side walks variety rather than paid-for organized entertainment. I have tried to instil in my children an appreciation of the outdoors and what there is to be observed if you only take the time to notice.

Socializing and the obligatory events that one is expected to attend, such as work functions, have always been difficult for me. I know that the anticipation in advance of such events is usually disproportionate to the actual event itself. Often I have boycotted events after getting in such a state about them in advance that I feel I cannot possibly attend them. However, I also know that once I actually get to such an event and become involved it is not as bad as I had feared, although I am sure that my idea of 'mingling' and socializing is not on a par with most neurotypical people.

As for empathy itself, I believe that I am able to recognize when a person is upset or there is something wrong. However, I am not always sure what to do or how to respond. It is certainly not a case of my being 'cold' or uncaring – quite the opposite. I think I am a very caring person and don't like to see anybody suffer, whether they are close to me or not. Not knowing how to respond also applies to other situations where I am not quite 'in' the conversation or on the same wavelength as others. It is likely that I will be aware that something is not quite right, but I won't be at all sure what exactly is wrong or how to react to it.

I would say that any lack of empathy displayed on my part is likely due to my not recognizing the need for it, or not understanding the situation, rather than any deliberate attempt to ignore or not acknowledge the need for it.

I don't like noisy, brash people. In the past I have usually found someone I can make friends with but they tend to be independent types who have a strong sense of themselves and who don't 'follow the crowd'. I suppose they are the other people who don't 'fit in'. My relationship with Sandra is based on common interests; we both like being by the sea, listening to music, reading, walking and we have similar values and senses of humour. We read together as Sandra likes me to read aloud to her, which I enjoy. When we are out walking with a flask of tea and a snack we are probably at our most relaxed and happy in each other's company. When we met I found out how much Sandra loved the moors and being out walking. I also love being outdoors and by the coast so this is how we got to know each other well.

We don't always share the same taste in music and we read different types of books – but we both like discussing what we read and what we watch on TV with each other. Both our fathers were prisoners of war in Burma and came from working-class backgrounds. This is another thing we have in common which helped us to become friends. Having the same kind of upbringing and values makes us closer.

Sandra is not a very conventional person. She likes time to herself, as do I. But I know she also needs people more than I do. I am happy if she wants to spend time with other people and would never stop her from seeing any friends because I know it's something she needs. We look after each other and I like her to be happy.

When Sandra gets stressed, I get upset too. I try to help the situation if I can but it does unsettle me. I try to calm Sandra down if she is very stressed by being reasonable and trying to help. However, if she is angry with me, I distance myself from it by going off somewhere alone. Sometimes I have to leave the house to calm down but this doesn't happen often.

When I get angry while out driving it's because people are driving very badly, behaving stupidly and showing a lack of manners. That upsets me a lot. I perceive it as bad behaviour and think it's ignorant of those people. I don't tolerate fools gladly!

There are some things Sandra does which really annoy me, like talking at inappropriate times such as when I'm watching the TV weather. This is important to me and Sandra knows this – but often forgets. Sometimes I become moody or bad-tempered when she does this but I don't think my bad mood lasts very long.

I realized very early on after we had met that Sandra was 'worth pursuing'. We wrote to each other a lot by email in the first months and I didn't want to lose her. Sandra told me that on our first date I talked too much and didn't pay her enough attention! Luckily, Sandra's younger daughter told her to give me another chance! I think our relationship keeps on getting better as time goes by.

Tony Attwood's Commentary and Q&A

Sandra tells us that when Victor's behaviour has upset her, she hopes that he will work out why without her needing to explain this to him. Instead, what generally happens is that Victor does not understand, withdraws further into himself and the situation deteriorates.

Having the expectation that your AS partner will somehow 'figure out' the reasons you are upset can often be a step too far for them. You could compare this with sending a child to their room to 'have a think about what they've done'. The child could be in their room for days – and still be none the wiser as to the reasons you might be upset or what to do about it. Victor is not going to work this out by himself because he is not wired to do this. There needs to be a different approach: the AS partner needs to have the problem spelled out.

Sandra goes on to say that Victor has *'difficulty in empathizing'* and that she feels like *'the adult partner who has to explain everything regarding our emotional life together'*. Yes, in a sense, it can feel as though you are an adult relating to a teenager. Within this relationship, Sandra has already recognized how very important it is for the neurotypical partner to maintain friendships with fellow NTs. For many NT partners, socializing is their lifeblood, it energizes them. It may be that they were renowned for this before they met their AS partner. A common issue is that the NT partner's social network, connections and life diminish over time and may eventually disappear altogether. The neurotypical partner needs to be aware of this and actively work against it. One of the ways this is done is through spending time with NT friends.

Often, close friends and family members notice the changes in the NT partner before the person recognizes it themselves. Comments like 'the light seems to have gone out' or 'you used to be so happy' might indicate to the NT partner that, whilst trying to adapt and compromise for your AS partner, that process has resulted in you losing your sense of self. The hope that, as an NT, your AS partner might become NT, is unrealistic.

Sandra then talks about how good Victor was with her when her mother died. He was gentle and held her while she cried. He was also very helpful in a practical way when she had a hip replacement. She says he *can "do" empathy when he knows what needs to be done'*. That is exactly the point. Victor was able to see the tears when Sandra was crying. He could see her hobbling about when she had her hip replacement. In other words, when a person with Asperger's syndrome *sees* (recognizes) the need, they can, and will, do all they can to help. This may even be one of the reasons you fell in love with them in the first place – because of their ability to help in a practical way. That ability to go out of their way to help on a practical level may also have given the impression of kindness and generosity – but *only if* they can read the need. The problems occur when they don't – and when they don't respond as you anticipate, you accuse them of lacking empathy.

Sandra makes sure she speaks to Victor in a calm manner and, now that she has learned more about AS, she checks herself and tries not to raise her voice when she's getting frustrated about something with him. It can really help an NT/AS relationship when both partners have an understanding of AS and the NT partner is prepared to make these sorts of adjustments.

Sandra's comment *'If I even sniff in an angry tone of voice, he'll withdraw'* highlights an odd contradiction in AS behaviour. The AS person may not be very good at reading facial expression or body language or determining when somebody needs compassion and affection. Contrarily, they can also be incredibly over-sensitive in perceiving negativity from other people that isn't there, or even intended. So it can appear that the moment you become irritated or annoyed, this is somehow amplified back onto you. It can feel very much as though you are treading on eggshells when the AS partner is so defensive. Saying anything that is not entirely positive (or sometimes just stating facts or being realistic) will be construed as criticism or negativity – commonly, this results in the NT partner suddenly becoming the focus of negative feedback or criticism.

Sandra says there is a *'big blank'* in Victor's ability to understand when he's done or said something hurtful. Again, if he can't see it, it doesn't exist. This is either that he can't read it or you have hidden it. In other words, you have to be very clear. For example 'What you have said made me feel upset. In terms of sadness, it is a 9.5 out of 10.

When I am a 9.5, you need to get me in a better frame of mind. Have you any suggestions? If not, I will tell you what to do.'

Another poignant comment Sandra makes is *'it's tricky to remember this all the time, and also I don't want to treat him like he's so different that I have to act like I am someone else'*. Yes, this is hard. It is asking you to act in way that doesn't feel as though you are being true to yourself. It is up to each individual to decide how many compromises and sacrifices they are prepared to make for that relationship to work. For many, the compromises result in the relationship being a good one – for both partners. It is the relationships where each and every compromise requires the NT partner to give up a little part of who they are – without receiving anything back – that are most at risk.

Sandra states here that *'I like the fact that I'll never really know him fully'*. This reminds me of a lovely phrase from an NT partner: 'In my husbands' autobiography there will be chapters I will never read.' There are certain parts of your AS partner that you may never know about or understand and that are never explained. For Sandra, this is something she has considered and it is not a problem for her. But for those who hope, as their relationship continues, to really get to know more and more about their partners, it could become a major issue. Sandra and Victor have a good, sexually intimate relationship. This is wonderful, but is not the case for many AS/NT relationships. Sandra and Victor have struck gold in that sense.

Sandra goes on to talk about Victor's relationship with his children. Though he loves them very much, he has a hard time empathizing with them. When we talk about empathy, it isn't an area that is only going to affect the NT adult in the relationship, it will affect children as well. Victor may not really understand their emotional needs. They may sometimes feel that 'Dad loves the "special interest" more than me', that he's more interested in his hobby than the children's success at school, relationships, and so on. As a child in that family, you learn not to talk about feelings. What that sometimes means is that children visit their friends and wish that their parent with Asperger's syndrome were more like the friends' parents. They won't necessarily understand why they are not and cannot be. It is important for an AS parent to be interested in their child's social and emotional life and to learn when they need affection and support.

Victor talks of his earliest memories of feeling different and finding life difficult as a child, describing how he would *'swing furiously'* on the garden swing. What Victor is doing here is resolving emotional problems with a solitary activity. He is not having to disclose his feelings to anyone or relate to other people, and it's likely that he would have found comfort in the rhythm of the swing.

Victor says he believes he is able to recognize when a person is upset but is not sure what to do or how to respond. This is interesting when you compare Sandra's earlier comment that Victor doesn't appear to realize when he is becoming stressed or anxious and needs to be told. A person with Asperger's syndrome will commonly respond to others by doing what works for them. For many, solitude is a major emotional restorative. Therefore, logic tells them that if they leave you alone, you'll get over it more quickly, so they'll keep out of your way. Another example would be if what makes them feel better is doing things – they will then do something they know you will appreciate as a way of making you feel better; the washing-up, cleaning the car, making you a cup of tea, etc. It is almost as though they try to repair your feelings by a practical act that's an expression of love without realizing that you are seeking a sense of empathy, sympathy and support – not a practical solution.

Cars and driving seem to be a common catalyst for explosions for people with AS. Why is this?
It's because they have a great desire to correct errors and when other drivers make mistakes or behave stupidly, they feel compelled to respond. The concept of intelligence and stupidity is central to Asperger's syndrome. The worst insult is to be called stupid. The problem comes for the car's passengers. The angry AS response to other drivers creates a huge amount of negative emotion, which destroys the atmosphere inside the car. One minute everything is fine and you're happily watching the scenery, and a minute later you find the whole mood has changed. It can seem very much as though the AS driver has one rule for themselves and another for the rest of the world. The trouble is that an irritation expressed so visibly can contaminate the whole family atmosphere.

Sandra talks about getting caught up in feeling emotionally different or wrong. Why might the NT partner feel this way?

The NT partner's first reaction is going to be self-blame. This is because the AS partner is so convincing and insistent: 'You're the one with the problem', 'You are crazy', or even 'You're the one with AS'. Having made so many mistakes and social blunders throughout their lives, deflecting is a comfort mechanism. Because AS thinking is black and white, it leaves very little wiggle room to accept some of the blame or admit fault. One of the greatest challenges for those with Asperger's syndrome is to admit they've made a mistake and say 'I'm sorry, I was wrong'. It's so rare.

Why does it take someone with AS so long to say sorry, if at all?

Sandra is right in assuming that the length of time it takes Victor to apologize following an argument is necessary processing time for him. Sometimes the AS person can work out what to do, and other times they won't be able to, regardless of how long they take in trying. Often, an apology might be written rather than face to face but, however it comes, if at all, it will take time.

Following diagnosis, is it unusual for an AS partner not to take an interest in understanding about AS, its impact on personal relationships and finding strategies to help improve relationships?

No. In fact it's very common. Basically, you've raised a problem they didn't think they had and so it's up to you to find solutions. This can seem arrogant, but there is also a lack of understanding by the AS partner on how having more information could help things. This is in stark contrast to their work or special interest, where they may be renowned for getting every single bit of information they can on that subject. But of course, in that case, it will be completely impersonal – just facts and information to do with a project or work. So the AS person can often feel that they have no need to do this, you'll do it for them.

6

Employment

Employment

RON'S STORY

My life has been one with a chequered work, school and social history. Since I can remember, which is now over 55 years, I have struggled with something that, until I was in my mid-50s, I had no idea existed. That something is Asperger's syndrome, the high-functioning form of autism that affects less than 2 per cent of the population.

Growing up in the 1960s and 70s, few people knew about the conditions I have. Teachers, parents and friends only knew me as highly intelligent but with a propensity for under-achieving. Indeed, my Grade 4 teacher wanted to hold me back a year because she saw me associating with kids younger than me, which she thought meant that I was underdeveloped. More rational heads prevailed and I was into the next grade. The tests that were conducted on me showed a slight lack of coordination and nothing more.

Fast-forward to 1998, when some acquaintances showed me what the signs of ADHD were in adults. I took my life story to a psychiatrist and the diagnosis came through: I'd had ADHD all my life. Suddenly, much of the previous 40 years of my life fitted into place. I now had a reason why my work, school and social histories were so erratic. My diagnosis helped explain why I could not hold down jobs for long and why I had few friends and a poor self-image. But that was not all. More was to come...

In 2011, after a long road from job to job, my wife suggested that I see a therapist for my problems with depression, anger management and other issues that threatened our relationship. We were tired of me holding down a job for just a few months or weeks – something I had originally chalked up to my ADHD and nothing more.

Even after the ADHD diagnosis and knowing how to better adjust my work habits to fit my jobs, there were still problems staying employed. For over 30 years I had moved from one low-paying job to another, trying to find a niche that I could fit into. For over 30 years, I had also not known that there was one thing that kept people from keeping me on as an employee or as a friend. It was the fact that I have Asperger's syndrome.

Asperger's is comorbid with ADHD and other conditions, implying that the regions of the brain that affect one condition also affect the other.

Growing up, I was never treated differently to other kids or my sister. My parents knew that there was something going on, but felt confident that I would triumph over all due to my resilience and intelligence. They never lost faith that I could amount to something one day. It was not merely a 'miracle' that I survived intact, it was the fact that nobody gave me any concessions or special treatment and it was expected that I could do the same things as anyone else.

As I entered adulthood, taking advantage of others to get work is something I could not do as I feel it demeans a relationship. And I respect myself far too much to do a job that could jeopardize my health. Gaining work through friends and family saved me a lot of grief. There is something to be said about having more than one set of eyes looking out for oneself.

Relationships are an area where I have learned from others. I have seen long-term relationships fail due to the most insignificant reasons as well as much more serious ones. The lessons learned by others gave me what I needed to cultivate and find a spouse who thinks like me with regard to making a relationship work.

My parents came from a generation that never knew the levels of divorce that people see now. The thought of leaving over things that could probably be worked out never entered their minds; it just wasn't done. They instilled in me the common sense to try to succeed with what I had. Having seen how marriages fail, and failing to keep my own previous long-term relationships intact, gave me insight into how to make this one work.

First, I listen to my wife. From the moment I saw Daria, I knew her to be a person with deep common sense and a good upbringing. That means I take into account her reasons for doing things and why she takes me to task for what I do and do not do.

She listens to me too and doesn't belittle my feelings or reasoning. Our arguments rarely last more than ten minutes and we never carry them on into the next one. Arguments are not usually about who we are but about other things that trigger our anger. We sometimes take it out on each other, which is irrational, but human nature. Once we get to what is really behind our feelings, we discuss how to resolve the situation and move on. It sometimes takes a few tries before I understand what she wants from me, but then I do the best that I can.

The other factor that helped our relationship is that I went into therapy, at Daria's recommendation. We both went initially, to get things sorted out between us. That led to her suggesting that I speak with a psychologist who specialized in diagnosing adults on the autism spectrum. Once I did that and the diagnosis was confirmed, the last of the parts of my puzzled life fell into place.

Yet I was still not able to hold down a job, which had been the bane of my existence for decades. Each year I would be worried about either losing my position or being forced to quit due to lack of mobility. And without fail, every other year, I would either lose my job or quit out of frustration that I was not 'getting anywhere'. The AS diagnosis enabled me to apply for and obtain government disability funding as well as disability tax credit.

Being retired has its problems with regard to our relationship. Right now, the living room and dining room are filled with my stuff, and that bothers Daria. But there's a reason my stuff is cluttering up the place: we have a boarder living downstairs and it's too cold in the basement. My office is filled up with the stuff that was originally stored where the boarder is now living. I realize that this sounds like a poor excuse, but I need a space that does not require any prior set-up before I can work on things. We are looking into other options, including a heated and insulated 'man cave' in the back yard.

The last job I had was perhaps the best one I had in recent years. Yet, like many others, it has gone. Unlike the other jobs, I had the advantage of having a job coach/advocate who could persuade the employer that hiring me would be a good thing – condition and all. Having the agency speak on my behalf gave me mixed feelings. On the one hand, I was confident that my skills would be useful to the company. On the other, letting them know about my condition (I refuse to call it a disability) meant that I might be treated differently.

I made the mistake of telling people about my ADHD diagnosis over a decade ago, and that led to me losing a job. I call it a mistake because I did not know how to tell people properly, and that led to other things going wrong, like relationships falling apart. Had there been someone with professional credentials fighting my corner, I suspect that things would have unfolded differently.

Yet, in the end, I still lost the job I gained through the agency – and under the most unusual of circumstances. For months they did not phone me with any shifts. When I went in to ask around six months later, they announced that, several months earlier, they had hired someone else. It would have been nice of them to tell me of their decision. I would have understood.

Disclosure is a two-edged sword. The good edge is getting people to understand how you work and reassuring them. The bad edge is that even after letting people know about the condition, they may still not 'get it' and treat you with either disdain or fear, having heard stories of meltdowns or violence. Educating people about the autism spectrum is tough and, when it comes to work and other important areas of life, doing it wrong can backfire. My own tendencies towards meltdowns have diminished considerably since 2011. Even before then I was placed on medication that has kept me on a more-or-less even keel.

Whenever I get deeply into a project I tend to forget time, though I still am aware of my duties. Despite people seeing me sitting at the computer for long stretches of time, I am always 'getting to' the other things. In the back of my mind, I know I have to get chores done but, in the moment, I feel I still have the time to do them. Daria sets me right when that happens.

One thing that sets our relationship apart from others is the fact that we understand where each other is coming from most of the time. Daria also understands the dynamics of ASC/ADHD and is willing to work with them instead of against them. We know that there are things I do that are not absolutely under my control, like hyper-focusing and procrastination. But we also know that there are things I can control, like spending money (which I try to keep reasonable). It is all down to understanding my and our limits.

I know that the time for me to work is pretty much done. After the age of around 45, it is far more difficult for people who have not had a steady career behind them to get work. We end up with the low-end jobs, and that gives employers a lowered opinion of us. Therefore, we have less chance of getting any job.

All in all, the years I had going from job to job, field to field were beneficial in one respect: I got to see changes in the workforce firsthand. No longer was I able to step into a job with just my hard skills and résumé. As time went on, soft skills and the ability to socialize became more and more important to employers. It was no longer about what you could do, but about how you got along with others. This is the sad downfall of nearly everyone on the autism spectrum.

Since employers are looking for the 'perfect fit' (whatever that may be), many seem to lose sight of the end product of the job; what it actually means to do it. People with ASD don't have much of a chance in this regard because their focus is usually on the work process and end result of the job, rather than who gets along with whom. Left to their own devices, most Aspies would love to just sit in the corner doing their jobs with little to no interference from co-workers at all. That means not needing to talk about upcoming contracts, no mention of the weekend or whether someone's kid is playing hockey at 6am on Saturday.

All we need is three Rs and four Ts to do our jobs:

- Remuneration

- Respect

- Responsibility

- Training

- Tools

- Time

- Trust.

These are what I call the 'lucky seven' and people who get those from their employers are very lucky. For my own part, the jobs that I felt gave me these were few and far between. The rest were survival jobs. I never knew what it was like to move up the corporate ladder or have financial and job security.

Above all, the most important thing I feel that Aspies need is to be trusted to do the job and to be respected as people. Far too long in most of their lives they have been belittled and shunned. Working in an accepting environment goes a long way to making their lives better. Employers get much more out of them too when that happens. That is why it is important for trust to be present in a relationship as well. That, and above all, love.

People merely see the outside of Aspies, not our inner feelings. That is why so few of us can socialize effectively. Daria once told me that when she met me she thought I had no emotions. I know I do, but they rarely come out as vividly as in others, nor as often. Which is one more reason I have had such a rough time of things. People cannot see the 'me' inside. Many feel that I am cold and distant. Although I may be distant at times, it is not for lack of emotion. I just feel that it is not always appropriate to show it.

This also explains why I never liked to socialize with co-workers: it does not leave me the opportunity to leave work behind at the end of the day. It prevents me from living my life as a private person. It also puts me more on my guard as to what I say, do and think in the presence of my co-workers after work is done. I feel that I cannot voice my opinions or do things that I want to do without being judged.

I hope that my insights carry some weight and can help others find relationships that last.

An NT Perspective

DARIA'S STORY

Autism has been an interest of mine due to a close family member being diagnosed in the late 1970s. I developed an interest in psychology when I was 13 and spent that summer reading psychology textbooks. I graduated from high school and later college with honours. As I could not afford university, I focused on gaining the experience I would need to build my career. My college diploma was in Medical Assisting and I started off working as a secretary in a number of medical offices. I then started working in home care and then in security. After that, I got into the IT industry and was well on my way to a management position, which is what I have always wanted to do. I had always worked well with people as well as computers and found that my strength was in building systems and motivating others.

In 2003, I started volunteering with a few autism societies. I attended fundraising dinners, delivered keynote speeches and participated in conferences. At the same time, I became a member of several online autism support groups for adults on the spectrum. I learned a lot about the challenges associated with being an adult on the autism spectrum from them. One of these challenges seemed to be getting and keeping a job. In 2004, I became the organizer of a local meet-up group for adults on the autism spectrum and learned from the participants that there were no work, financing or therapeutic programmes in place to support autistic adults. I talked to people at the residential programme I was in and they told me that '[they] don't do adults'. As soon as a child reached the age of 17 they were out of the programme and the family had to make other arrangements.

While I may not be on the spectrum myself, I have developed an understanding, appreciation and acceptance of the autism spectrum over the past 15 years. I do my best to work around the various challenges faced by my husband and others on the spectrum.

In 2009, I began applying for work in the not-for-profit industry. I joined the board of directors of a local autism association that was focused on providing better quality of life for individuals and families of people living with autism. Some programmes for teenagers were already in place, and individuals on the spectrum were seeking assistance. Word of our meet-up group began to spread throughout the professional community and some staff members would attend. All of them were amazed that there were no services for adults with autism and Asperger's syndrome. They began helping adults on the spectrum to work with their situations, for example by applying for jobs under their comorbid diagnoses. It was not long before agencies in town began providing services for adults with autism spectrum conditions. The first was an employment agency that helped people with intellectual disabilities obtain work. Eventually, our association helped launch an IT consulting organization that hired people on the autism spectrum, as well as a programme to help younger adults learn how to work with others and obtain employment.

I met Ron, the man who would eventually become my husband, in the spring of 2001. We were driving to another town for an event, and I found that we had similar interests in books, music and movies. It wasn't long before we were dating, and we were married in 2004. I knew that he had always had problems with keeping jobs and that he had been diagnosed with ADHD in his mid-forties. By the time we were married, he had an excellent job as a digital librarian. He loved the work, was good at it and was paid. We bought a house and, a week after we moved in, Ron was given notice of a lay-off, which was devastating for him. He was 50 years old and it was difficult for a man his age to get another job.

Ron always accompanied me to meet-ups: while I spoke with concerned parents and spouses, my husband always socialized with the adults on the spectrum, and fitted right in! I began noticing other things, such as resistance to showering and brushing his teeth, texture issues while eating, obsessive behaviour, special interests and an explosive temper. Ron said that shampoo and liquid soaps felt gross in his hands. I had to tell him to take a shower every second day. Ron's temper became evident after he was laid off. Prior to that, it almost seemed like he had no emotions because he would not react to situations like other people. He was on antidepressants, which I assumed was the reason why he seemed to have no emotion. His mother told me that his temper had always been terrible and he would often fly into rages. The loss of that last job shook him up, and I noticed that he would lose his temper over the smallest things.

He applied for other jobs and worked for temp agencies after the lay-off but could not hold down a job for more than a few weeks. He would be 'let go' due to his behaviour: he didn't take the job seriously or he talked about morbid things or he did not seem to like working with women or he was writing down complaints about his job on his computer (as a way of coping) and got caught. We got him involved with an employment agency for people with disabilities, but they were not used to working with such a 'high-functioning' individual. They expected him to be able to keep a job if they found him one.

Money was tight without a second income coming in, and I ended up working three jobs before taking a job at a non-profit that paid well. Ron kept looking for work and his temper got worse. The last straw was when he supposedly went to work with our neighbour one day and I found that the neighbour was at home sick. I asked him where Ron was and he said he didn't know. When Ron got home, I confronted him and he told me that he had been fired from his most recent job after only a few days.

Ron claimed employment insurance so that something was coming in. When that ran out, he threatened suicide, and I knew that something more needed to be done. I got us into couple's counselling and it was found that we had no issues relationship-wise. However, it was identified that Ron's defence mechanism was to apologize for unhelpful behaviour to cool things down and then to carry on as before! I was told that I needed to take him to task for his behaviour and hold him accountable. I also told Ron that I would be happy if he never worked again as long as he looked after the house. I have an auto-immune disorder which saps my energy, and my work took too much out of me. Fortunately, Ron was OK with doing the housework and I was relieved.

The issue with his temper was resolved because the trigger had been his constant search for work. Being allowed to stay home and do what he liked, while being responsible for the house, seemed to relax him a lot. At times, he would start to slip when he was heavily involved in one of his projects, but I would remind him of the agreement and tell him that I was holding him accountable. He'd then get back on track. Once in a while I still need to remind him, but that will always be the way and we've accepted that. I know not to show a lot of emotion, even when I am furious with him. He once lost his temper because his computer would not start, and he smashed the glass on one half of our glass-top dining room table. By the time I got home, he'd cleaned everything up and was honest about what happened. Surprisingly, I did not lose my temper. When we argue, I let him express his emotion and then we sit down and I calmly ask him what it's really about. We then talk about what is really bothering us, we resolve it and we move on.

Unfortunately, we were still short of money. I could not take on any more jobs without making myself sick and I was not going to have Ron look for work. I contacted a local autism association and they helped us obtain food. A friend of mine was a retired psychologist who specialized in autism. She agreed to assess Ron, and she had us both write out what everyday life was like, and what Ron's experience was like throughout his life. After a few interviews, some testing and her reviewing the many pages of information that we gave her, Ron was finally diagnosed as being on the autism spectrum. The psychologist wrote a 29-page report and helped us complete paperwork for disability tax credit. We took the report to our doctor who used it to complete the forms for a federal disability pension. Ron was immediately approved for both, which ensured a monthly income for Ron and nice tax return for us each year. Ron would no longer have to pay taxes as he was now 'retired'.

The employment agency decided to see what Ron's success with work would be like if a job coach was involved. They successfully got Ron a part-time job at a printing company in our city and he did very well. The employer knew what to expect and how to accommodate Ron; Ron knew what to do and what not to do, and he got along well with everyone. For two years he worked part-time at the print shop while collecting his pension and we were finally doing well financially and within our marriage! Full disclosure in Ron's case was the best thing for him, as it has been for many of the adults in the meet-up group. Unfortunately, that job would also come to an end, although we wouldn't find out for a year. Ron was told that the company wasn't doing well financially so he would be called when there was work; he was not called for six months. Finally, I drove him over to the print shop and we found out that he had been let go without Ron being notified. They had found a full-time employee and did not officially let Ron go because the paperwork would have been a pain. They finally processed the paperwork and Ron got his Record of Employment. He has not been employed since, but he is still upholding his responsibilities around the house, and that works well for both of us.

We have been married for over 11 years and we have our ups and downs. What married couple doesn't? I've learned that when a person stops fighting against autism and finds a way to work with it, the results are amazing. Frankly, being emotional and expecting my husband to be different would be too tiring for me. It would have also killed our marriage. To make things work, we had to think outside of the norm and just do what was right for us.

Tony Attwood's Commentary and Q&A

This chapter highlights the learning difficulties and other conditions that often co-exist with a diagnosis of ASC – conditions like ADHD, dyslexia, problems with number skills, dyspraxia, as well as other personality disorders such as narcissistic, schizoid or borderline. So, sometimes the diagnosis of ASC is not the final diagnosis. The central theme may be Asperger's but there may be other disorders, secondary depression or anxiety diagnosed as well.

This chapter also deals with the very real problem for many people on the autistic spectrum of gaining and retaining employment. This holds all kinds of issues relating to finances and self-esteem that can put more pressure on a relationship already under strain.

Why can it be so hard for people with Asperger's syndrome to hold down a job?
Often this can be because of the social demands in that setting and the need, within most jobs, for flexibility in planning. Someone with Asperger's syndrome will often be very good in the areas of knowledge, honesty and thorough attention to detail, but, increasingly, that person is expected to be part of the team and engage in the social atmosphere and network at work, and this is where the challenges lie.

Ron received disability tax credit when he was finally diagnosed. How do people find out what support is available to them?
I think they need to go to whatever agency supports people with autism in their area and find out, through their helpline, where to go and what to do next.

Daria talks about the importance of not fighting against autism but finding ways to work with it. How important is that?
Yes, I strongly applaud that. If you try to fight Asperger's syndrome, the chances are you'll lose. It is better to work with it and steer it as much as you can. It's a bit like having a stagecoach that's out of control – you

can stand in front of the horses and you'll be run over, or you can jump on top of the horses, work your way back to where the reins are and then steer the stagecoach in a particular direction. So, I think it's better to work with Asperger's syndrome rather than try to hold it back.

How important is counselling for people with Asperger's syndrome and their partner?
I think it's essential, because otherwise you waste a lot of time trying to work out what to do. You do need a third party to provide guidance. The problem is trying to find someone who knows the area well enough to be able to do that.

Ron talks about having a 'man cave'. Is it important for a person with Asperger's to have a space that is theirs?
Oh yes. They need their sanctuary that the kids stay out of. The problem is when their sanctuary becomes the cure – the place where they feel so at ease that they never want to come out of it. So, short bursts in their sanctuary is the way to go.

Ron talked about a two-edged sword of disclosure. What advice would you give on who and how to tell?
As Ron identifies, a diagnosis can help or hinder in the workplace – that phrase that Ron uses of disclosure being like a 'two-edged sword' is very perceptive. Disclosure to employers is something that needs to be weighed up carefully and, as Ron mentions, needs to be done in the right way. It's about who needs to know and how much do they need to know?

People with AS are usually breathtakingly honest and duplicity is not easy for them. So, it is best to be honest. The question is how do you explain? What information do you provide to the person you're telling? It's almost as though, in the AS person's pocket, is a list of cards. Each card represents a different level of disclosure for a certain type of person. So if it's somebody that the person meets casually at work, it may be just a brief comment and sometimes you might not use the 'A' word, you just say 'I'm the sort of person who...'. So you can give the explanation as a description of personality, not necessarily a 'syndrome' that has all sorts of repercussions associated with it. You might say, 'I'm the type of person who is very blunt, sometimes I say the first thought that comes into my head and some people find this offensive, and I wonder if I have offended you? Please tell me if I have and I will apologize. I was not deliberately meaning to be rude.' It is important that the NT partner proofreads this statement to make sure it is wrapped appropriately for a fellow NT.

What advice can you give for people with AS in the workplace?
Talk to your NT partner. They may be able to perceive the situation better than you and give valuable advice regarding the social and emotional components of work. It is important for the AS person to debrief about what's happening at work and for the NT partner to meet the work colleagues, to know their characters, and then to be able to give advice.

7

Family Occasions

LAURA'S STORY

It was during the playing of a game of chubby bunnies that I glanced over at him, and my spirit withered a little more. As everyone else was either gaily stuffing marshmallows into their mouth or else looking on with smiles, laughter and shouts of encouragement, Ethan was staring at my engorged nieces and nephews with what looked like a mixture of contempt, detachment and disapproval. He was the ultimate party-pooper: the guest whom people make a mental note to cross off the next party-list. Except that he couldn't be crossed off – because I was married to him!

Prior to this jolly festive gathering, I was at the end of my ability to cope with Ethan's seemingly relentless lack of fun, sociability or manners. I felt I was losing the happy, sociable, fun part of myself as I was constantly anxious about Ethan's behaviour. I'd stopped enjoying social gatherings because, with Ethan in tow, they were just too awkward and tense for me. Before that Christmas party I'd told him that, unless he made an effort, that was it: the end of us. I was seriously thinking about us separating then and I've seriously thought about it since but, somehow, we've always managed to find a way forward together.

Being a sociable person myself and having been brought up to be polite and to always pretend I'm having a good time, even if I'm not, I found Ethan's lack of effort – or what often seemed like just downright rudeness – almost impossible to live with. This particular family gathering came at the tail-end of a Christmas in which Ethan had been as detached, grumpy and sullen as a moody teenager. All this despite it being the first Christmas my dad had spent with us since my mum died, and us having two young children to try and make it magical for.

Whilst we're on the subject of Christmas which, I understand, holds all kinds of trials and pitfalls for people with Asperger's syndrome, there's another, not so much occasion as custom that has caused tension in our family – that of giving and receiving presents.

Ethan finds it almost impossible to lie. This may seem like a commendable trait but, having lived through fifteen Christmases with him, I've realized how far happy relationships depend on lies – or at least things remaining unsaid. As in life, Ethan is fiercely practical about presents: if he doesn't like something, he feels obliged to tell the giver so that they know not to buy him that item again. I am equally fiercely emotional. I'd rather have a lifetime of dud presents than hurt someone's feelings and embarrass them by telling them that the present they lovingly chose for me is way off-mark.

I must admit to a slight triumph in this area though. These days Ethan will, if not feign delight at a rubbish present, at least smile and say thank you. This is progress. Ethan's dad, from whom Ethan has inherited most of his traits, is still downright rude when it comes to Christmas or birthdays. With him I think, in part, it stems from him not being able to handle the emotional demands that a present brings. He doesn't know how to express any kind of tenderness or thanks in return for the expression of affection that the present represents. The best reaction you can hope for from him if you buy him a present he really loves is that he will put his glasses on and examine it. Don't expect a thank you, or a smile. At worst, you'll get the kind of reaction I got when I bought him a scarf a few Christmases ago. As Ethan's dad opened the wrapping, the nervous tension in the room grew. He glanced at the scarf before asking gruffly 'What have you bought me this for?' and chucking it on the floor.

Ethan hadn't quite gone that far during that first Christmas without my mum, but he wasn't far off. His sullen silence spread a blanket of gloom day after day. If my mum had been there she might have said 'I told you so'.

Of both my parents, it was my mum who was initially most wary of Ethan. Not surprising considering the early encounters she'd had with him.

The first time she met him was for a family meal out. My elder sister and her family were there, along with my younger brother and sister, my mum and dad and some close friends. First off, to say that this was the first time that Ethan was meeting my family, his small talk was painfully sparse. He answered questions (when he heard and processed them) as briefly as possible and asked no questions in return. Even more mortifying, when the garlic bread came out which was, admittedly, a little overdone he made a grand display of whacking it on the table to prove how hard it was. He followed this up by complaining ungraciously to the waitress (something that made my mum recoil in horror). All I could think was that, on his first meeting with my parents, the quality of the garlic bread was more important to him than the impression he was making on them or the feelings of my dad who was paying for the meal for all of us.

Somehow, we were still together a year or so later, although I was riddled with doubts about the relationship. Ethan, who had no such doubts, managed to persuade me that he should come on our family holiday. I guess I saw a week spent together as an opportunity for my family, surely, to be exposed to some of Ethan's positive traits that had drawn me to him in the first place. But, just two days in, came the ice-cream incident...

On our way to the beach, we passed a sign that advertised a huge array of weird and wonderful flavours of ice-cream available at a little shop located about a ten-minute walk from the beach. So, later that afternoon, a group of us set off walking to the shop, debating what flavours of ice-cream we would try. However, on arriving at the shop, excited to place our orders, we discovered that the only flavour the shop had left was vanilla! Granted, it was a bit disappointing, but we all made the best of it and ordered our vanilla ice-creams (with chocolate flakes to lessen the blow!). Except for Ethan, who seethed with indignation and anger. He had a go at the girl working a holiday job in the shop and laboured the point about how we'd just walked for ten minutes – *ten minutes* (together, across a beautiful beach, in the sunshine) – to buy these ice-creams. He stomped out of the shop and walked silently back to our base on the beach, angry and unable to engage in any kind of activity or conversation for the remainder of the day. Once again, food – and its inadequacies – had won out over people and their feelings.

But, despite ice-cream-gate and countless other toe-curling incidents, seven years on from that ultimatum at Christmas, we're still together. Two of those years have been spent with a diagnosis of Asperger's syndrome for Ethan. I think that's the factor that's made the biggest difference for us.

Before the diagnosis I would interrogate Ethan after every social test that he failed, to try to understand his apparent standoffishness. His answers would always be the same: he didn't realize he looked so miserable or sounded so aggressive – that's not how he meant to look/sound; he couldn't hear what people were saying in all the noise; he couldn't follow what was happening; he found the whole experience so stressful/boring that his mind just zoned out. I generally responded to all of his explanations with contempt. His descriptions were so far away from anything I felt, experienced or understood that I just couldn't imagine that it could be true that another human brain could process things so differently from mine. He seemed to contradict basic human instinct. What could be so intimidating or overwhelming about hanging out with friends and family? In my more sympathetic moments, I told him that he just needed to learn how to be sociable – to try harder. In my harsher moments, I told him that he was talking rubbish, that what he was saying was ridiculous, that he just didn't try and that he had no manners. After a while, he stopped trying to explain.

And so life went on, until we genuinely hit breaking point. Ethan was drinking – a lot and every day – just to be able to cope with life. I was distancing myself, distracting myself from the unhappiness and emptiness of our relationship with other things – work, friendship and our kids. I regularly fantasized about divorce.

Everything came to a head when Ethan ended up in trouble with the police. Life came crashing down around us and Ethan was forced to address his issues. He went for counselling – which is where (and I'll be for ever grateful to this woman) the counsellor instantly recognized his traits and began the process that referred him to an autism spectrum diagnostic centre. His diagnosis, and my resulting research into AS, changed everything. I discovered that there were millions more like him – *exactly* like him. That, within the realms of AS, he was normal. Other people described exactly the same feelings, exhibited exactly the same behaviours. Surely all of these people couldn't be making it up. The possibility that Ethan wasn't just a rude, unpleasant person was tremendously liberating and hope-inducing. Armed with knowledge, there were now adjustments that we could both make to our lives and to our relationship to make life work better.

Since then, we've learned a lot about ourselves and each other. We're discovering all sorts of tactics that can enable both of us to enjoy life and function more effectively. Life isn't perfect and we still both cringe our way through some social occasions, particularly if Ethan is tired, has had a busy week or the gathering involves lots of people and noise. But, on the whole, we're doing much better by introducing a few new approaches.

First of all, we've told some of the people close to us about Ethan's Asperger's. This takes the pressure off for both of us. When we're with these people, I don't have to worry about Ethan saying something blunt or taking himself off to recharge for a while. And Ethan can relax more and be himself. I was initially worried that knowing he had AS might make Ethan sink further into his unsociability; that it would finally give him the permission he'd been seeking. But, actually, the opposite has proved to be true. Knowing about his condition and understanding himself and the challenges he faces has made Ethan work harder to live better. The words he spoke the night before he went for assessment spoke volumes to me. When he told me that he was feeling nervous about the results, I presumed he was worried that he would have Asperger's, along with all the implications that would bring. Actually, the reverse was true; he was nervous that he wouldn't – that there would be no explanation and therefore nothing to be done about his behaviour, because he genuinely wants to be a nicer, more sociable person. We have been selective in whom we've told. None of Ethan's family know, although most of my family do and a few of our friends. Having spent his whole life trying to fit in, Ethan doesn't want to burn all his bridges by proclaiming to everyone that he doesn't. But, at the same time, he's given me permission to tell anyone I feel I need to. And I'm really grateful to him for that.

Second, I go to things on my own sometimes, or agree in advance that Ethan will leave early or slip away for half an hour to recharge. Sometimes I feel a bit sorry for myself as a result, a bit conspicuous when everyone else is there with their husband or partner, a bit envious when other people's husbands are chatting easily – jollying everyone along and generally being the life and soul of the party while I make excuses for my husband's absence and single-handedly manage our three lively children. But then I remind myself of the alternative. If Ethan were there, he wouldn't be like those other husbands – he wouldn't be chatting amicably. He'd be struggling to hear, to make sense of or know where to interject in conversations. After a while, he might give up altogether. And, rather than being able to relax and be sociable myself, I'd feel stressed, on edge and embarrassed about Ethan. After years of fights, arguments, tears and frustration, I've realized that it just doesn't work for Ethan to come to every event – family or otherwise – that we're invited to.

The fact that he's excused from coming to everything means that, at the events Ethan does come to, he generally makes a concerted effort. Knowing that I understand what being with people all the time takes out of him, I think, makes him feel better. I try to ensure that he doesn't get overloaded and that downtime is built into his day. Sometimes it's hard, when he's in a dark room playing on his computer and I'm managing the kids' homework, making tea and at everyone's beck and call. I might not have Asperger's, but sometimes I'd like some downtime too. At times I'll get resentful and drag him out to help. But I try, when I can, to allow him the time to recharge – for all of our sakes.

The final lesson I'm still learning is not to trust my interpretations of Ethan's looks and behaviour. Ethan looking or sounding fed-up, critical, miserable or annoyed doesn't necessarily mean that he is any of these things. Sometimes when he sounds aggressive, snaps at me or looks angry or vacant, he is genuinely surprised that I get upset. He has no idea that he's come across that way. I'm learning not to react to his reactions. I'm also learning, and slowly accepting, that he's not like me! The natural expression on his face is never going to be a relaxed and happy one. He's always going to overreact to little things that other people would barely notice and, most of the time, conversation will be an effort for him. He's not like me. And I need to stop measuring him against my 'normal'.

I also try not to compare us to other couples. I struggle sometimes when I see their sociability: how easy it is for other couples to connect, how other couples and families always seem to be doing things – holidays, nights out, Sunday afternoon walks – together. I have plenty of friends, but they remain just that – *my* friends. As a couple, Ethan and I do not have many other couples that we connect with and do things with regularly. In some ways I feel held back by Ethan, but part of what attracted me to him in the first place is that he is different to other men. He thinks deeper, tries harder and lives in a realm different to the mundane, everyday 'society' rules that surround us. Being with Ethan also gives me permission to take off the mask and not to have to pretend or make the effort all the time myself. I'm allowed to not want to talk. He doesn't get offended if I want my own space to do my own thing – even if it's the only night we've got together that week. What Ethan presents is totally genuine – no frills, no polish, no smooth-talk. He doesn't remember people's names – even people he's known for years, or what job they do. But he'll help them out if he can. He's real and rugged and he's giving life – on a strange planet amongst people who are not like him – his best shot. And I love him for it.

One generation on from his dad, Ethan's Asperger's has been diagnosed. Ethan is taking responsibility for understanding himself and being the best person he can be, within the constraints of the symptoms he lives with. He's willing to accept when he's messed up and to attempt to try harder next time. And I'm learning to accept that he's very different to me and that isn't always a bad thing. Together, we're learning to live together differently.

An AS Perspective

ETHAN'S STORY

As I drove down the motorway with my two small children, wife and father-in-law packed into the car with me, the feeling of trepidation built in my stomach. My rare visit to Bristol could only mean one thing: Christmas – a happy time of year where families get together and have fun. Apparently. We were on our way to my wife's sister's Christmas party where eleven children and fourteen adults would be crammed into an extended semi. Before we walked through the door, Laura warned me that I'd better make an effort or that was it (we'd already had an argument regarding my lack of enthusiasm about the situation). However much I didn't want to be there, I didn't want to upset Laura. So I put my happy 'making-an-effort' face on and went inside.

The first challenge was to say 'Hello, how you doing? Have you had a nice Christmas?' to all the adults (not the children, I didn't know what to say to them). Twenty minutes in and I was exhausted. My smile started to hurt so I stopped it. My sister-in-law had two cats and a dog and I found myself counting animal hairs. There was lots of food on the table. And while the children were examining it by touching and sniffing, I was deciding what I wasn't going to eat.

By this time the noise level was getting as high as the temperature, which was also rising. I was trying to make small talk, but I found it difficult to hear what people were saying so they were mainly short conversations. Everyone was then gathering in the sitting room where they were going to play a game, but this game wasn't what I was expecting. Kids were stuffing their faces with marshmallows. I didn't get it. To me this didn't seem like a game, it just seemed like an excuse to eat more sweets. That made me judge the quality of the children's diets and question the parents' decision making. I saw Laura glare at me and realized that I mustn't have been meeting acceptable standards. I knew Laura was annoyed with me and that, somehow, I was letting her down.

But I really didn't know what to do to make things better. I didn't want to be there, and I suppose it must have shown.

All this, however, was not the first time I'd got it wrong with my new family. The first time was at a family meal out.

Picture the scene: Laura, my future parents-in-law, two sisters-in-law (one with a husband) and a brother-in-law, plus a couple of other random people I didn't know. All sitting in a noisy restaurant waiting to meet me for the very first time. Laura was more nervous than me, and I knew I had to make a good impression. But I didn't have a clue what to say. I was really hungry and all I could think about was when the food was going to arrive. When it did, I was pretty underwhelmed. The garlic bread was over-done and there was hardly any of it. As I didn't have anything else to say, I picked a slice up and tapped it on the table saying 'Wow, this is well done' – because it was. I was making a point and, I thought successfully, breaking the ice all in one – creating a comedy moment that we could all be involved in. It seems though, that I wasn't very successful in communicating the comedy element. Apparently, I wasn't smiling when I hit the garlic bread on the table. In fact, I'm told I looked really hacked off. And I suppose I was. We'd paid for a decent meal (well, my future father-in-law had) and we weren't getting it. It wasn't right and that's all there was to it. So I complained and we got some replacement garlic bread. It never occurred to me that this might have upset anyone. Why would it? I wasn't blaming them.

Following my apparently shaky start I thought it would be good to get to know the extended family better by going on holiday with them to Devon. So I asked Laura if I could go. Laura's family were very different to mine, they chatted about stuff and had a laugh. One day on the beach a group of us walked to what promised to be an amazing ice-cream shop with hundreds of unusual flavours. All I could think about during the walk was what combination of flavours I was going to experience. On arrival there was a massive sign proclaiming the full list of exotic ice-cream flavours from apple crumble and lemon meringue pie to white chocolate chip cookie dough. But, to my horror (and I was horrified) we were told that they had sold out of everything apart from vanilla. I was devastated, which soon turned to anger.

'Why haven't you removed the sign from the front of your shop?' I asked the girl serving us (it was a removable easel type sign so wouldn't have been hard to do). I suppose I had a bit of a go at her. But I felt like I'd been lied to and I couldn't hold my frustration in. In my head, people around me just disappeared. I wasn't thinking about what anyone might be thinking about me. It was just me and the situation. I wouldn't – couldn't – think about anything or anyone else.

Fast forward to post-diagnosis and everything has changed for me. I wasn't cured, I was enlightened. The revelation that I *was* different took me to the highs of 'I can work with this, get the tools and function as a "normal" person', and to the lows of 'Why me? I'm disabled, disadvantaged, dysfunctional, and just plain weird.' I understood why I didn't have any close friends, why I didn't click with anyone. Things to me were more interesting than people. Over the last four years since diagnosis, I now treat social situations as going to work. I know my role – I've practised it enough, and I know what job I need to do. Like work, I sometimes enjoy it. I make eye contact, try to smile, ask questions and, most importantly, try to acknowledge with replies to show that I'm listening rather than just guess what the appropriate response is. It takes more concentration, but gets better results. In the past, when I couldn't hear people I would just say a very generic reply having no idea whether it was the right reply or not. Usually this terminated the conversation. Now if I don't hear someone I'll usually say pardon, although in a noisy pub my chances of hearing them even if they repeat themselves is pretty minimal.

When a social event is over, I feel that I have accomplished something – like I've just made a flat-pack wardrobe. Then it's time to go home for a rest. Since the diagnosis, this is something that I can do more. Laura understands that I need downtime between social interactions, and knowing that I can get this helps me to feel less panicky and to try harder during the times that I know I need to perform.

Tony Attwood's Commentary and Q&A

Laura talks about Ethan being the *'ultimate party pooper'*, and this is common with Asperger's – not understanding how to resonate with or enhance the happiness of other people. In fact, people with AS expect other people to be within a very narrow band of emotionality. This relates to not being able to handle the emotional demands that a present brings. With AS adults, what you have to do is to actually teach them what's required. You have to explain something which, for others, is a very basic interaction skill expressed since early childhood. You also need to use this as a learning experience rather than a criticism.

Laura talks about how she stopped enjoying social gatherings with Ethan because they were too tense. This is common, as is the NT partner attending events alone. You may then have a feeling of disloyalty or disappointment by not going with your AS partner, but it depends on whether you want to enjoy it or not. My view is if you go without them, you'll probably enjoy it more and they'll probably prefer to be at home alone far more than they would enjoy attending the party.

Now, just to address the lack of awareness that the AS person has about how they are coming across – yes, that's a common characteristic. As Laura recognizes, *'The natural expression on [Ethan's] face is never going to be a relaxed and happy one.'* I'd say that's the case for most people with AS. Neurotypicals view a still face as a miserable face, and yet the person with AS may be feeling perfectly happy. It is what I call an 'emotional dystonia'... that the AS face doesn't show emotion easily and you can't necessarily read the inner feeling of an Aspie from the superficial or non-existent facial expressions.

The final thing I want to say is that I agree with Laura's statement that she needs to stop measuring Ethan against her normal. This is important, otherwise she's going to be terribly disappointed and frustrated.

Is being 'too honest' – about presents among other things – a common issue for people with AS and their partners? Can people with AS really not see when it would be tactful to pretend or, at least, to remain silent?
Oh yes, this is a common problem. One of the things we do diagnostically with children who may have Asperger's syndrome is to describe someone saying thank you for a present they didn't like and then ask the child 'Why would she say that?' An Aspie child will say, 'I don't know. If she didn't like it, she didn't like it. She should say so and then she won't get it again.' You see, neurotypicals tend to focus on people's feelings often as a greater priority than telling the truth. Aspies generally don't do that.

Laura ends by mentioning some positive aspects about Ethan's personality. What are some common positive traits of people with AS and how can these be celebrated more within relationships?
Loyalty, honesty, integrity and predictability. All those sorts of things can be very important in a relationship and are things that the Aspie generally has bucket-loads of. But these traits may also be incredibly boring ... I mean in the sense of the happiness of the NT partner. These attributes may not be enough to make up for the lack in other areas of the relationship.

Ethan talks about how he *'wouldn't – couldn't – think about anything or anyone else'* apart from the ice-cream. Is it usual for people with AS to have such tunnel vision? What problems can this cause in a relationship? Can it be turned into a positive?
Well, that tunnel vision is great in a work environment because the person with AS will be still there at 10 o'clock at night and they'll get the job done. So again, many of the characteristics of Asperger's syndrome are valuable in a work setting. The problems occur when you put these traits within the family and relationship dynamic. There are roles and expectations in a family, as a partner and as a parent, that are not necessarily intuitive to the AS partner and that challenge their 'tunnel vision' approach.

Ethan refers a few times to not being able to hear people, particularly in busy surroundings. Is this a common problem for people with AS?
Yes, it's called central auditory processing – that ability to focus on one voice when there's lots of background noise, especially lots of background chatter. What a typical person does is, as I'm talking, your brain focuses on my signature voice, the way I talk. Then if the radio or other things are going on in the background, what you do is you amplify my signature voice and turn down the 'voice' of other people. In Asperger's you often can't do that. So it's not a sign of deafness, it's central auditory processing – being able to focus on one signature voice, amplify it and reduce the volume of other voices. That's one of the reasons why crowds are so stressful for people with AS. There are just too many people, too much movement, too many sources of noise.

Ethan's interpretation of the garlic bread incident is very different to Laura's account. Laura talks about not being able to understand Ethan's brain or way of thinking. Can people whose brains are wired so differently ever hope to really understand and empathize with each other, never mind giving each other what they need?
'Ever hope to really understand and empathize with each other...' I'm not sure how achievable that may be. It's like winning the lottery. Some people do win it, but the vast majority don't. And, in some ways, although it's nice and comforting to imagine what a relationship like that might be like, you've got to get on with the reality. That means both sides of the partnership making a constant and conscious effort to understand the other and meet their needs, as far as they can. And to accept that there are and will always be differences, but to find ways to live and even thrive, within those differences. And there are lots of practical ways of doing that, as this book explores.

8

Finances

DAN'S STORY

Julie and I have had many arguments about finances over the course of our marriage. These are generally not about a shortage of money which stops us living normally or even, by most people's standards, very comfortably. These are about a lack of openness and communication. Julie is very patient in that she will keep coming back to the topic and has been very resilient in dealing with my resistance. I realize that this is an indicator of how strong her love for me is, not that she is trying to irritate me, but sometimes the visceral reaction gets the upper hand, even now!

Julie is a very enthusiastic and encouraging person who has always been kind and supportive of me in our relationship – something I generally have not reciprocated. I tend to see the risks in things rather than the unmitigated opportunity. Her enthusiasm is one of the things that I love about her, but I often find it quite frightening and overwhelming when it takes over. It is also difficult for her that I do not build her up in the same way that she does for me – something I know that I have been poor at doing.

I have always been self-reliant about money. That does not mean that I am always careful with it, but I do understand that in our relationship having it, or a shortage of it, is down to me to deal with.

As I was growing up, my father had control over the family finances. He was the only breadwinner and it seemed perfectly natural that he should determine how money should be dealt with. We were well off and so the issue of money as a limitation did not feature much. As a teenager, I took holiday jobs to earn some money for myself. My father used to question my spending, which I didn't like. This led to an agreement that I would manage my own money, an arrangement that we kept to from then on.

In my first marriage, we pooled money for household and other shared costs, but retained the rest for ourselves. This continued when we had children too. Whilst I have always been happy to provide and share my income, I have never been in a relationship before where I have not felt that I have had my own 'me' money. The income I have always been lucky enough to have has never required compromise on the basics, such as accommodation and food, etc. Julie does not have paid employment and therefore the income for our lives comes from me. Because I am the one in our relationship who is responsible for delivering this and dealing with any financial needs, I naturally want to have input into how the money is managed. If this sounds a little controlling, it is not meant to be, any more than a statement of practical fact. I see the job of being the breadwinner as one of my major contributory roles in our relationship.

Julie has said that, in the past, she has not felt fully aware of our financial situation. This has not been due to deliberate secrecy on my part. I feel it is due, partly, to a lack of consistent attention from her. Because I work in finance in my professional life, I do not wish to spend considerable amounts of time managing personal finances in my leisure time. I have always kept a mental picture of my financial position and have been fortunate enough that I have not had to be too detailed. That does not work so well if there is someone else using the money, unless there is some coordination! Therefore, we have an arrangement whereby Julie receives a monthly amount for personal use and housekeeping. This worked fine for a while but, a couple of years ago, I was about to pay a tax liability from a rental income account which Julie has control over, only to be told that much of this had been spent without any reference to me. Julie will sometimes overspend her monthly income and ask for more without explaining where it has gone. I find this annoying when I feel that I am having to account to Julie for my income and expenditure. I do have a tendency to get defensive when she questions me, because I feel that I am required to justify my access to the money I have earned. I know that it is 'ours', but that does not change my instinctive reaction, although I am learning to control it and I do realize that Julie is not seeking to attack me.

I feel that Julie has not always understood the factors affecting spending and that money we have might be earmarked for something, such as the tax example. These situations have improved through explanation and discussion and I realize that I need to explain rather than make assumptions about her (or my) understanding.

My understanding of Julie's concerns is that she does not trust my judgement or my motives and feels that perhaps I will somehow leave her financially in the lurch. It is perhaps these concerns that have led to the situation that we now experience where her attitude has provoked a negative reaction from me, leading to a further lack of trust on her part. The cycle needs to be broken in order to make things better and to improve mutual understanding. I can understand why she feels like this because I have spent money on some fun things– see the example below – but she does not understand why I feel that I need to do this.

My professional life is as a Finance Director and I have been successful in this career. As a result, I feel it devalues me when my wife implies, and sometimes states explicitly, that I cannot manage money. I do not think that she is trying to be insulting about this, but a lack of balanced comment has led to a build-up of feeling that she really believes I am not good at something that I have made a successful career out of.

We had a period a few years ago where my income fell substantially very quickly and we had to re-mortgage the house in order to pay some debts. Whilst this was stressful it should be taken in the context of a house that had been fully paid for and was a circumstance of the economy rather than one of financial frivolity. I was not good at explaining this to Julie, for whom this period was very stressful. However, the episode has resulted in a far more economical lifestyle.

Notwithstanding all the problems that I know I have caused by not being completely open about money, I recently acquired another car without telling Julie. She, quite rightly and not surprisingly, was angry and very upset.

I have spent some time thinking about why I do this. I think it is caused by four things. The first is the point mentioned earlier – that Julie clearly feels that I cannot manage money. Based on my career, this is clearly untrue. My behaviour is to some degree a reaction to that.

The second issue is that I quite often feel that I do not really get any enjoyment out of my income. I work hard, I work away from home, and I feel quite lonely a lot of the time. Whilst my income is quite high by many people's standards, much of it now goes on our new house, where I do not spend much time or have much involvement. As I am mostly away, I feel a bit removed and, when tired, I am resentful that the fruits of my work are being translated into something that I am not really directly involved in and cannot fully enjoy.

The third reason is that I do not want to feel that I need to account for everything I spend. I do not expect Julie to account to me for all her expenditure from her monthly amount and, as the provider, I do not expect to be made to feel that I should do this when I meet the normal household costs and other agreed outgoings.

The last reason is, for me, the most difficult. Julie has told me in arguments that I do not bring much to our relationship other than money. She is referring to friends and social life, which is more important to her than to me, partly because I spend most of my working days talking and interacting with people to the point that I want 'me time' in the evenings, whereas she does not do this to the same degree. I know that she is right and that she does bring most of our social life into our relationship, and I do love her for doing that. She is so much better than I will ever be at social relationships, so it makes a lot of sense to me that she does this.

However, I think that my behaviour stems from resentment about the charge of not bringing much to the relationship. I see it as devaluing something (earning money) that is important in enabling us both to do the things we want to do and is the thing that I spend a huge amount of time doing. When I hear that I don't bring much to the relationship (whether this is actually said or not), I forget all the positive things that Julie has done for me and focus on the offence to me, which is very painful for her and, I know, unfair of me.

I am lucky in that I love my work, but that does not mean that I would continue to do it if I had equivalent resources without needing to work. In my mind it seems bizarre to me that, while my financial provision is not considered an important contribution to our relationship, me taking some of that financial contribution for something I am interested in appears to be very important. This sounds a bit petulant, even as I write it, but I believe that I do contribute hugely to our relationship by enabling Julie to do the things she wants to do without having to work. I feel that I should be able to get some direct enjoyment from my labours as well as providing for our marital household. I think that what I need to have is recognition that my working does contribute hugely to the material quality of our lives. The logical me realizes that the problem for Julie is not that I use the money but that I never discuss it with her first, but my instinctive actions are a kind of sullen – and generally subconscious – response to not feeling valued.

I feel that we need to re-base our joint stance on finances in order to resolve this situation. I want to be reassured that my contribution to our relationship is valued so that I, in turn, feel valued by contributing to our lives together, rather than looking to find some self-worth by buying things for myself. I need to provide Julie with reassurance that I am not habitually seeking to mislead or somehow undermine her or our relationship. Our lack of full communication on finance issues has pushed both of us into fairly entrenched positions so that a balanced discussion about a way forward has become difficult to have.

We have developed some strategies to manage the financial 'reporting'. We have a spreadsheet that we each use to input our expenditure so that we both know what is being spent. This covers the running of our homes including mortgage, utilities and improvement expenditure. I have undertaken to get the mortgage on our new home paid down in priority to other things, which I have not forgotten, notwithstanding the car issue.

Julie has been very tolerant, despite her frustration. I love her and I want nothing more than to enable her to do the things that she wants to do. This is the rational and true position, but it sometimes gets distorted in arguments or in situations where one or both of us are tired or otherwise distracted. I would never seek to create stress for Julie as a result of financial matters. It is true to say, however, that our priorities are different. I realize that, for her, the issue is one of trust and betrayal as a result of not communicating, rather than the spending of money. I have never previously thought about this in those terms and can see why she would be unhappy with some of my expenditure without us having talked it through and me explaining the context.

I love Julie – she is core to my life, despite how it must appear to her – and I would never consciously seek to make her feel insecure any more than I would do that to myself. Clearly, I have failed at this but I am trying to learn to think in advance about my actions so that this does not happen. I do not know the extent to which Asperger's impacts on my attitudes to money. I do know that in a work environment I am very communicative and go to great lengths to ensure that I communicate appropriately. But that is in a work and not a domestic setting. I know that I have the capacity to be resentful of criticism that I feel is unfair. I can deal with this at work, and maintain objectivity, but that is more difficult in a marriage or personal relationship. However, awareness is a big part of the road to working out a better way and I believe that we can achieve that.

JULIE'S STORY

Throughout my childhood, although I wasn't conscious of it at the time, money was tight. By my teens, I was aware that our family lived on a budget and couldn't afford such extravagances as eating out or holidays abroad. To do anything special meant planning ahead and saving.

At 17, I started the process of becoming financially independent from my parents: moving away from home and starting work as a student nurse. If I wanted something I couldn't afford I had either to save for it or have a talk (which you could do face-to-face in those days) with my local bank manager.

By the time I met Dan, we were both aged 40 and I had been a single mum for 12 years. I had raised two teenage sons, worked full-time and owned my own home. Besides occasional help from my parents for the maintenance of my car or for help with the cost of school trips for the children, I managed my own money and was financially independent.

Though money was always tight, I managed it well, always aware of my income and monthly costs, only once getting into 'serious' debt (around £2000 back in 1995). I owned one credit card, paid my bills by direct debit and, whenever possible, put money into a savings account, either to put towards something special like a holiday or, more frequently, for emergencies such as repairs or unusually large utility bills. In short, I knew the state of my finances at any point in the month and didn't imagine any responsible adult would live differently.

Before Dan and I married, I tried several times to bring up the subject of how we would manage our finances. Should we have our own accounts along with one joint account into which we both paid and from which all our bills were paid? Or, since he earned substantially more than I did, maybe one of us should pay the mortgage and the other the bills? Should we set up a separate account for savings? These conversations, always initiated by me, were uncomfortable and would be shut down by Dan as quickly as he could manage.

When we married, Dan was keen that I should give up my job to be able to spend more time with my family and, in particular my parents. We had sold both our homes and invested similar amounts (£125k and £150k) for the cash deposit on our new home. After we married and had moved into our new home, whenever the issue of money was raised, Dan's tone, manner and even body language would change. He would instantly raise his voice and become irritable and accusatory. Instead of having a calm discussion, every attempt to talk about money ended up in a huge argument – and usually with me in tears.

I would repeatedly try to explain that, as his wife and partner and as responsible adults, we both needed to know what our financial situation was. How, otherwise, could we know what our limits were or what savings we could put aside? How could we plan for our future? Somehow, every conversation became about me being unreasonable or stupid for not understanding what he was telling me. After a while, I felt unreasonable and stupid – and I eventually stopped raising the subject at all because it just became too stressful to do so. I felt worn out and defeated.

Ironically, Dan works in finance and generally seems to enjoy his work, which commands a very good salary. Having given up my full-time job as Dan suggested, I was happy to have, for the first time in my adult life, the opportunity to spend some time doing things that didn't necessitate my being paid, and it wasn't long before I decided to set up and run a charity. Dan encouraged and supported me throughout those years. Looking back now, I realize that having no income made it much more difficult to feel justified in raising the subject of money. What right had I to question our income or spending if I wasn't contributing? Dan would say that I didn't need to know anything about our finances. He was the breadwinner and he would therefore manage the money. I was given a monthly allowance for food and petrol and any other 'incidentals'.

Then something tipped the balance that brought our finances sharply into focus. At some point within five years of buying our first home together we had been in a position to almost entirely pay off our mortgage. This took the pressure off us financially and would have been a wonderful opportunity to talk together about our plans and saving options. That never happened. Instead, almost immediately, money was borrowed against our home to invest in a business owned by an ex-colleague of Dan's. A few years later that money was lost.

A few years after that, a year of unemployment led to us being further in debt. Because Dan had already drawn down money against the house for the previous investment with his friend, he was unable to take out a further loan on our home. Unable to pay off or consolidate debts and unable to get further credit, Dan turned to me to help, insisting that the only option was for me to sign up to a joint loan to pay off the debts. I felt bullied and left with no other choice. The stress culminated in me giving an ultimatum – I needed him to be completely transparent with regard to every detail of our finances: credit card debts, incomings, outgoings, etc. If I couldn't have these, I would leave.

I could see how hard it was for Dan to share this information, and it was not pleasant for me to feel that I had been left with no alternative but to demand the information and threaten divorce. Despite the bleak outlook at that time, sitting down to discuss our finances together was the first time I felt we were equal partners. During the discussions that followed it became apparent that one hobby of Dan's – cars – had eaten a hugely disproportionate amount of income. The amount spent on just one of those cars was two thirds of the total debt we were in at that time. Dan's point of view was that he earned the (only) income and should therefore be able to spend it on whatever he pleased without reference to me.

In all of these conversations Dan was hugely defensive, always responding as though he was under attack, irrespective of how sensitive or diplomatic I would try to be. No amount of trying to convince him that we were a team helped allay his fears. It was as though we were speaking different languages. The talks also highlighted our different value systems – mine being relationships, sharing and planning for a future together, his being the acquisition of what I referred to as 'stuff', material possessions. I accepted that we needed money and a certain degree of 'stuff', but he did not feel he needed to share or plan. Not sharing our finances meant we never discussed plans, even short term, let alone retirement.

Dan would say that I don't value his contribution to our relationship (primarily money) but this is untrue. He believes that that is what I am saying when I talk about money – because he seems only to hear the negative or critical aspects of any conversation. I find it frustrating and depressing that he is rarely able to recall any of the positive things I say to him. Yet he will frequently relate, verbatim, any words of encouragement he has been given by work colleagues often telling me the same story several times.

As we got out of debt and Dan found another job, all financial control reverted back to him as he changed passwords on the accounts, making it impossible for me to access them. I became increasingly lonely and depressed and felt unable to articulate clearly to friends or family why this was.

It was a year later when I heard, for the first time, the term Asperger's syndrome. Reading through the list of typical AS behaviours was a lightbulb moment for me. With both of us wanting our marriage to survive, we went down the route of getting a formal diagnosis, first of all visiting our local GP and then being referred. I started to read and learn more about AS. It has always surprised me that Dan, even four years later and having had a diagnosis, shows no signs of interest in the subject at all. This, despite the fact he has identified other family members he believes are also AS.

I understand now that what previously appeared to me to be different value systems with regard to the importance of money versus relationships may not be as clear cut as that. Could the problem be a combination of typical AS difficulties with theory of mind (his inability to understand how I feel or think about how things might be in the future), problems with executive function (planning, regulation and cognitive flexibility) and his increasingly high levels of anxiety and subsequent need to control his environment, his love of routine, dislike of change and inability to understand context or to see 'the big picture'?

I recently discovered that Dan had started down the route of acquiring yet another substantial purchase, again, without any mention of this or discussion with me. Our previous experience years ago and the consequences of that do not seem to have made him consider how this purchase might impact on me, or on our marriage. There never seems to be a learning curve. It's as though he can compartmentalize his life so that I am not privy to anything he thinks I would not condone. It feels like another betrayal of trust.

I still love my husband. I would love advice from someone who knows and understands AS, with all its limitations, challenges, possibilities and potential. Could there ever be a solution that would allow us both to feel more secure and trusting and less anxious whilst not having to compromise what makes each of us who we are as individuals?

If not, then what?

Tony Attwood's Commentary and Q&A

When we look at Asperger's syndrome in its broadest sense there can be issues with what we call daily living skills, and people with AS can have major problems in organizational planning and especially, as an adult, with financial arrangements. There is a tendency to be one of two extremes: either entirely Scrooge-like or to have no real idea of the need for financial planning at all. This then means that the neurotypical partner has either to live with someone who exercises complete financial control but is mean when it comes to spending or, if their AS partner has absolutely no idea about finances, has to try and take control themselves and sort things out. In this area of finances, it also makes the AS partner prone to predators, as they are likely to take on board what people say rather than being able to discern a person's character or personality. People with AS don't have a built-in radar to discern who the guys are that will make them sign away the family fortune. They are very gullible and vulnerable in that sense, and the daily living skills of budgeting can be a real problem for them.

'...she does not trust my judgements or my motives.' Yes, this is because the NT realizes the risk of addiction to that special interest in the AS partner's life. They can be compulsive, buying for the sheer thrill of maintaining the special interest and the collection. It not only provides enjoyment but a sense of self – determined by possessions rather than who they are.

'Julie clearly feels that I cannot manage money. Based on my career, this is clearly untrue.' My answer to that is that there is a difference between career and home life. In a workplace or within their career the AS partner may be able to behave quite appropriately in terms of budgeting. They may even be renowned for making logical budgeting decisions. But, when it comes to the home, and the special interest comes into the equation (which isn't there in the work setting), there is an overriding and almost irresistible urge to spend on the interest.

Julie has told me in arguments that I do not bring much to our relationship other than money. She is referring to friends and social life, which is more important to her than to me, partly because I spend most of my working days talking and interacting with people to the point that I want 'me time' in the evenings.

In other words he is saturated with socializing. As far as he's concerned, he's had enough and just wants to be by himself. Now, whilst this feeling of needing 'me time' is completely understandable, there may also be needs that the NT partner or the family has, children that need tending to, etc. For the relationship to work for both of you there has to be a compromise. This could be: 'Well, OK, you can have 30 minutes of "me time" but after that, the buzzer goes, and you are back on duty as a parent.' The AS partner must recognize the need to switch their role from being a person at work, a person having 'me time', a parent before the children are in bed, and then a partner to their husband or wife. So it is working on that understanding of everyone's needs and finding a compromise that works for all.

'I do know that in a work environment I am very communicative and go to great lengths to ensure that I communicate appropriately.' Once again, Dan is referring to his work situation. It can be extremely hurtful to the NT partner if it appears their partner is able and motivated to communicate successfully at work but doesn't make any effort to do so at home. It may feel as though the AS partner can communicate, but at home has chosen not to do so.

Julie talks about Dan becoming irritable, angry and accusatory during discussions about money so that, eventually, she stopped trying to discuss the subject. Is this common?
Yes. It's common because the person has learned through the years that if they keep going and bullying, eventually people will give in. The ability to compromise and negotiate is very elusive for those with Asperger's syndrome. Neurotypicals are always working on compromise, trying to understand each other's point of view. Whereas the AS way is to keep going until you, the NT partner, gives in. As you are likely to become emotional during this process, this adds more power to the AS argument and eventually you are forced, by fear of either actions or retribution, to relent or do as you are told.

So in other words, people with Asperger's syndrome need to be taught the skills of negotiation and compromise. It doesn't come naturally. This is what is commonly taught, and learned, in friendships – particularly those of any longstanding. You learn negotiation, compromise and problem-solving as a group or as a team. But if you have never experienced that, then you have never learned it. Most children learn these skills in primary school, but if they reach adulthood never having acquired those skills, it can feel very much like dealing with a child in situations where negotiation and compromise are required.

In your experience, is it common for the AS partner to want to retain control and privacy over their actions? Why is there such fierce independence?
Because you might change the decision! You might make them do what they don't want to do, so their reasoning is 'Why should I tell you? You'll only say no. If you don't know about it, then you cannot say no and I can get away with it.' If they don't tell you, you can't stop them or make them do something differently, so it's worth the risk of the consequences of being found out. It is very self-centred. Also, although there may be an awareness that this tactic might make things worse in the long run, that's another day. The decision not to tell is a quick fix for the moment. The frontal lobe, which is responsible for organizing, planning, time management, etc. is not responding and so the AS reaction is impulsive. The AS partner will say what you want to hear. For example, if asked 'Have you put the rubbish out?' the answer is immediately 'Yes'. When, actually, the AS person knows that you'll find out later they haven't – but it means that for now they can carry on with the computer game or special interest.

It seems a common factor that AS partners crave 'things' over relationships. Why is this?
Because 'things' don't change their minds. They don't say no. People are emotional and unpredictable. It's another reason why many people with AS like pets – they give unconditional love and acceptance. The problem for people with AS is that having 'things' can become addictive. Often a person with AS will say, 'You don't understand, you just don't get it.' In other words, you don't understand the value of the special

interest in that person's life. Sometimes the feeling for the NT partner is that the person they are in a relationship with is more in love with their special interest than their partner. There is a lot more emotion, time, dedication and happiness associated with the objects, the collection and the interest than there is in the interpersonal relationship, which is very hurtful. There is also the issue of not learning from experiences, because there is never a 'Plan B'. There is only a 'Plan A'. The 'Plan A' can be dormant for a while and then it comes back and is the default position. It is very tempting for the person with AS to go back to what is familiar, what they believe in and know, without thinking of the long-term consequences. It is living in the now. Neurotypicals have the ability to see consequences for decades ahead but the AS person may not pick up on that. What can be infuriating is that the person keeps making the same mistakes because they don't have an alternative way of dealing with it. They only have the default position.

How important is it for both partners to have an awareness of their impact on the relationship?

This is very important. But the NT partner needs to be able to convert their thoughts and feelings into Aspergerese for the person with Asperger's to understand. It is a foreign language. I think you need to have an agreed code that may involve numbers or cues (such as the traffic light system referred to in Chapter 3) that both people understand. So you've got the basic emotions of happy, sad, relaxed, anxious, affection and anger... and both partners rate where they are on each of these dimensions between 0 to 10. It's a very simple way to help understand each other's feelings. However, be prepared for the partner with Asperger's syndrome to rate their feelings to two decimal places.

Why might someone with Asperger's syndrome find it hard to talk about financial plans?

This is because sharing means losing control. There is the need, in the AS partner, to control because, without it, there is the danger of being challenged on how money is spent. What if the NT partner tries to curtail what they want to spend on, for example, their special interest? You would be spoiling their fun – and it is the greatest fun they have in life. If they didn't have that, how on earth would they cope? It is their antidepressant.

Cars are clearly Dan's special interest. The AS partner may prioritize expenditure on the interest as though they are addicted to it because it gives them a sense of extreme pleasure. It is what I call intellectual orgasm, which feels far more enjoyable that any interpersonal orgasm. So money for the special interest may often be considered a greater priority than budgeting for the family. Unfortunately, the AS partner may blow a whole load of money on the special interest and leave the NT partner with the responsibility of picking up the pieces afterwards. But it's not just financial, the NT partner may find they are not included in discussions about certain major decisions of the AS partner because, if they share, they lose control. So they may ensure they are the ones to decide where you live, what you do, etc. This area of control and money is why, for men with Asperger's syndrome, life was a lot easier a hundred years ago because it was a very male autocracy. In certain cultures today, where male autocracies still remain, it is easier to be an AS male because your wife has to do what you say. But in many European and North American societies that is no longer the case. So not being included in decisions (until the wheels, metaphorically, fall off) can be a major problem. It is hard for the NT partner who can never feel secure and trust that the finances are as they should be.

If the person is able to use strategy and planning in their workplace in order to sustain and grow the company, why would they be unable to see that planning is essential in a domestic situation – even if only to sustain their special interest into the future?

Because here you are using logic. When it comes to the special interest of someone with AS, it is emotional and they are not good at emotion. In other words, they are making an emotional and not a logical decision. So at work they can make a logical decision about the financial arrangements of that company, and that's fine. But when it is their special interest, they are in love with the interest – and love is blind, so they don't make rational, logical decisions, they make emotional decisions.

Is there a way in which an NT partner can help the AS partner understand that lack of planning will ultimately lead to the death of the relationship?

I think the only way, if you are going to stay in that relationship, is to be quite draconian and say 'You have to do this'. No negotiation. It is just a matter of 'You can't...' The NT partner has got to be authoritarian, which will be hard for them as it is not their natural personality. They have to say 'Which part of "no" don't you understand?' It is very difficult to do but it is the only way to get through it in terms of keeping the relationship together. 'No, you can't buy it, it's not allowed.' Being in that authoritarian parent role is not easy. You are supposed to be in an adult relationship where you're both being reasonable and able to come to this agreement together. Yet instead you feel more like the parent of a wayward teenager than a partner

In this case, you are talking about the issue of trust in a relationship. Whilst it may be purely in regard to financial matters, trust in the area of finance is important within a relationship because it determines what you can and can't do. Commonly, the person with AS will not recognize their actions as the breach of trust that it is, and so the NT partner will have an uphill battle trying to get any understanding or movement forward on this.

The NT partner must remove all emotions and say logically 'This is why we have to make this decision,' and 'That is why we are going to have to keep to it' in an unemotional and practical way. Despite the protestations and toddler tantrums, the NT partner must stick to the ultimatum. Because the person with AS will sulk and complain like a child that doesn't recognize why you won't give them a chocolate bar, as they don't realize that they're morbidly obese.

9

Intimacy

RACHEL'S STORY

I never thought much about intimacy until I met Chris. It just happened, part of the unfolding of each day when I was with a long-term partner. However, I know now that intimacy for me goes way beyond the physical intimacy of sex; it is the looks and touches of affection throughout the day, shared smiles and the sense of being listened to and understood. It is someone to share my joy with and someone to sympathize with me when I am low. It is something my AS husband cannot do.

Initially in the relationship, however, Chris did seem able to do this. We didn't live together and he was absolutely obsessed with me. I realize that now. It really was an obsession, but at the time I just thought he loved me. After we married, everything changed. Work became his obsession again and my need for intimacy went unmet.

Our undiagnosed AS/NT status hugely affected our relationship. For years I thought the only possible reasons for his behaviour towards me were that he was stupid, that he was thoughtless and selfish or that he didn't love me. Clearly he is not stupid, so I swung between thinking he didn't love me, often that he didn't even like me, and thinking he was a selfish uncaring man.

I spent years feeling unloved and disliked; it felt like even my presence in a room annoyed him intensely. Sometimes I felt like he hated me because of the way he spoke to me. He contradicted me, interrogated me and often reduced me to tears. It hurt most of all when, after our daughter was born, he was utterly unavailable and unsupportive.

However, as soon as we got into bed he would want sex. If I asked for a hug from him during the day his hands would be under my clothes and he would want sex – even if I was upset about something. The lack of intimacy in every other area of our lives meant I resented this deeply. I felt like I was only wanted for sex, and it turned me off completely. Sex pretty much stopped.

It doesn't help that I have endometriosis so sex is often uncomfortable or painful, however, that's never been an issue in other relationships; I just deal with the pain. However, with Chris, at that time, sex wasn't something I wanted anyway. It felt like another chore, another demand at the end of a demanding day, so the pain put me off more than before. All I wanted was a loving cuddle without any demands, and it broke my heart never to have that.

In all honesty our sex life had always been unusual. Initially when we met Chris said he'd never kissed anyone before and that his only previous relationship had not been good sexually. It was with a woman who was as old as his mother, and the only reason he was with her was that she had suggested living together as they were both so lonely. I found it easy to believe that sex was not great.

Kissing was an issue pretty much from the start, which I initially put down to inexperience. It was clumsy and often his lips would be pursed and he would put them outside mine, so it felt like being kissed by a remora fish. Also he would kiss very repetitively, over and over again for the same amount of time and in the same way, like a metronome, and would end up with his nose squashed into my face. Even lining himself up to kiss me appeared to be difficult. He finds distractions, such as music, difficult, and I find that that makes the issues with kissing worse. After a few years I just gave up.

Chris also has a very particular way he needs to be touched in order to feel any sexual pleasure. Oral sex does nothing for him as he can hardly feel it. He has to be held very firmly and in a very particular way and sex only works for him in certain positions. Over the years I've noticed Chris has very little awareness of how to move his body in certain ways and has, for example, only learned to hop at the age of 49. The missionary position does not work for him as he can't make the movements that are needed. This is the case with some other positions too. With all of those aspects, along with the need for positions that give particular stimulation, we are quite restricted on variety. It's also hard to remember not to touch Chris's skin lightly anywhere, especially over his stomach as he's really sensitive there. We now have hugs where I don't move my arms and just hold him very tightly, sometimes rocking from side to side. This is described as a stimming hug by some people and can be very comforting for someone with AS. One of the saddest things for me is that Chris struggles with eye contact and it's really strange to be making love with someone who is staring fixedly into the pillow to the left of your head rather than into your eyes.

However, there are positives. Chris does like and want sex and kissing, which seems unusual in AS, and he also brings his perfectionism and attention to detail to the process, which can be wonderful. He is very willing to try things if I suggest them and to do things I like but that he doesn't, for example massage. He does not like to be massaged himself but will try to massage me. It's a strange thing that, although he is an engineer and an artist and can do really intricate work with his hands, he struggles to give a massage that is not repetitive and clumsy. There are so many paradoxes.

Since the diagnosis of AS we are learning all the time and things have improved beyond recognition. For example, I have learned that his behaviour does not necessarily mean he dislikes me, and he has learned to modify this so that I feel more cared about. As our communication has improved, we've been able to discuss things like kissing without it degenerating into an argument, which is a positive step. We are able to be more honest and open about what we want sexually, which is important when one partner cannot give or pick up non-verbal communication. It's odd having to be very explicit verbally about what works and what doesn't, but it's effective. I learned that Chris had actually kissed people before – but not anyone he was in love with, so he felt it didn't count. Also, in his previous relationship they usually had sex at least five times a week, sometimes every day and that was what he thought of as normal. With a young child, a house and endometriosis I simply cannot live up to that. Finding out about these things made me very sad and is a good example of how AS can affect a relationship, as his view of the world is so different from mine. He uses the same words but with completely different meanings. Through talking, I have found that sex is often the only way Chris can express his love. Without it, he feels unable to show affection and is very sad and lonely. I am the opposite, expressing love verbally and with non-sexual touch. Without those things I find it hard to feel loved and therefore don't want sex. It's a difficult situation but, with imagination and a sense of humour, we can work around it.

I have learned that Chris does not understand or use body language, so had no idea that his behaviour was actually asking for sex without using words: he didn't mean it that way. He also has no concept of context, so something that is OK in one situation is OK in every situation to him. He can't see that it may be inappropriate in a different context.

The main things that have helped us are learning more about AS and developing better communication techniques. We are seeing a specialist counsellor. I don't ask too many questions and when I do, I pick a good time for them. I also just give information and don't try to chat. We use a traffic light system to communicate feelings during important discussions. So I will often ask Chris how he is feeling, on a scale of 1 to 10, where 1 is suicidal and 10 is the happiest possible. It's so funny how, from his behaviour, I'd have said he felt maybe a 2, and he says 'eight'! This positively affects the dynamic of our relationship completely as I now know he's happy being with me and that I'm not driving him mad. Chris has learned to help much more with our daughter, to offer to do more and to ask if I want a hug sometimes. Things don't work out so well if I'm stressed but, generally, they are much, much better. I am deeply grateful for the difference that the diagnosis and specialist help have made to our lives.

An AS Perspective

CHRIS'S STORY

To me, intimacy is the expression and sharing of love, passion and desire. Intimacy to me is about much more than sex.

I have often said 'passion' is a very important, almost defining, word to me. I feel life is about passion; passion in all things, passion *for* life. To really live is to feel passion and to feel passion is to live. To me, a life without passion seems empty and worthless. Passion for good food, for example. This need not necessarily mean extravagant, expensive or fancy – far from it. Enjoying scrambled eggs that are cooked fabulously well with bread that's perfectly toasted is a passionate experience – and heightened all the more when shared. Sharing an experience magnifies the passion.

I feel that intimacy is sharing a passion for each other and could be said to be the finest passion of all. As such, it is the ultimate passion that makes all other passions so much more real. Rachel once said 'Sex is the glue that holds a relationship together'. To me, intimacy is the passion that gives the other passions their meaning and 'flavour'.

A difference between Rachel and me is that Rachel has to have a finely balanced combination of positive emotion and physical wellbeing to be intimate. On the physical side, feeling stressed, tired, drained or having other commitments on her mind all dampen feelings of intimacy. Emotionally, Rachel needs to feel loved, valued and appreciated and to have a sense of emotional wellbeing in order to feel intimate. I have found this delicate balance can be quite difficult to achieve and some of this, I can now see, is related to my AS.

Rachel suffers from a range of conditions that also combine to make intimacy harder. Rachel has severe endometriosis. Without medication, this leaves her with chronic abdominal pain for over three weeks a month. Additional intense pain can leave her totally incapacitated – rolling around on the floor and close to passing out. This incapacitating pain can be triggered by sex or physical activity (e.g. running). The constant pain is exhausting for her. She manages the condition using hormone tablets but a side-effect of these is that they substantially reduce libido. Rachel also suffers from long-term depression, which has the classic side effect of, amongst other things, making her very tired. The medication for this can also have the side-effect of reducing libido and the desire for anything intimate.

We have a young daughter, and Rachel has left her career to be a stay-at-home mum and to home-school our daughter, Esme. This means that Rachel has little time to herself, except in the evening after Esme has gone to sleep. This couple of hours will generally be the only time we have the chance to be alone together. I work irregular hours (usually leaving in the morning when everyone else is asleep), meaning that Rachel does not get the chance of a break until I arrive home. All of this, combined, means that Rachel is more often than not very tired in the evenings. She is a 'lark' and feels best in the mornings. When stress and cumulative lack of sleep come into play, Rachel will understandably feel the need for a good night's sleep far more than any want for intimacy.

A contrast between Rachel and me is that I am a 'night owl' and come alive at night, even if I have had a very long and difficult day, which is apparently somewhat typical of AS.

Intimacy helps me feel better. I find it relieves stress, aids sleep and rest, lifts mood and eases worries. I suffer from 'cluster headaches' (debilitating and ferociously painful headaches) and even during an attack feel the desire for genuine affection and intimacy. I find it helps me at least cope with the attack and can even help alleviate it.

So we have a situation where I commonly feel alive and active in the evening and Rachel will be tired and run-down. These differences can mean I have, in the past, spent many nights lying awake into the early hours staring into blackness, my mind whirling with feelings of emptiness and undesirability. I can do nothing other than lie still, waiting for another day to end.

I am not sure if the way I feel (meaning, quite literally, the way that I 'do' feeling) is entirely due to my AS, but I suspect this must be a substantial part of it.

Some of the reasons I feel as I do I put down to the fact that Rachel is the first truly passionate relationship I have had. We met when I was 42, and I had spent my whole life up to that point longing for the passion and meaning to my life that I could never seem to find. I understand that a great deal of the reason for the path my life took is due to my AS (I have only just been diagnosed at the age of 49 and after being in a relationship with Rachel for seven years) and it is clear that there is an inextricable link here.

I feel the diagnosis has helped a great deal. We have been able to begin to improve our communication and better understand our differing needs and ways of thinking and feeling. From this, we are beginning to be able to help accommodate each other more effectively.

I think the main difference between the two of us is that intimacy for me is a cause of wellbeing, whereas with Rachel it comes much more as a result of wellbeing. I suspect this may, on my part, be related to the AS condition. Also, for me, if I am feeling low, a lack of intimacy, passion and desire makes me feel worse. I can see, particularly since the diagnosis and the resultant improved communication, that this has meant I have been less able to respond to Rachel's needs in the past. Conversely, Rachel first needs the emotional feelings of love, value, appreciation and wellbeing before she can become intimate. She also needs to feel physically able (i.e. not too tired) to be able to be intimate.

I feel my diagnosis of AS is making it easier to understand how we function differently and, with that, we can try to accommodate each other's needs more effectively. We are also getting better at recognizing when we may not be communicating well and are learning to check this. A small example would be Rachel asking me how I am feeling, physically and emotionally, on a scale of 1 to 10, as she often cannot tell from my manner. I might answer 'physically three' (possibly due to feeling ragged as it is the morning when I do not function well), 'emotionally eight' (as I will be feeling fine in myself). This is particularly helpful in putting her at ease as she may have thought I was cross, upset or ill, or was showing some other negative feeling when, in fact, I am feeling fine but may just have had something on my mind. This may be something quite inconsequential and not at all negative but it would appear my resultant 'far away-ness' can come across in a completely unintended way.

Tony Attwood's Commentary and Q&A

Early on in Rachel's story she says *'After we married, everything changed'*, and this is a common experience within neurodiverse relationships. It is almost as though the person with Asperger's syndrome has won the prize and they no longer feel they need to make any effort. You've signed the contract and that's it, there's no need to pretend any longer. The same can also apply in the area of intimacy.

Intimacy is split into three areas: verbal, emotional and physical, and the person with Asperger's syndrome is going to struggle with all three areas:

- Verbally, in terms of struggling to articulate their thoughts, or to know what it is their partner needs to know about them.

- Emotionally, in terms of having the vocabulary to express emotion. A characteristic of Asperger's syndrome is what we call 'alexithymia' – 'a' meaning absence, 'lexi' meaning words and 'thymia' for emotions. Often, the AS partner is emotionally inarticulate, and emotional intimacy is very difficult for that person.

- Physically, not only in the sensory sense but also in the 'choreography' of intimacy. Often what can occur is difficulty reading the cues for sex. For example, misinterpreting a hug as a cue for sex, or not wanting to receive a hug because they perceive that as you wanting sex when you don't.

So it is really about understanding the language of intimacy for both partners, and sometimes all the NT partner wants is affection, without affection necessarily being considered foreplay by their AS partner.

Rachel uses a lovely phrase, *'it felt like being kissed by a remora fish'*. One of the difficulties for the person with Asperger's syndrome is that, commonly, they have not had many romantic experiences or relationships. They may have no sexual history and may still be a virgin. Initially in the relationship, that lack of 'emotional baggage' can be very appealing to the NT partner. Generally, people learn about kissing and sex in their adolescent and teenage years with practice, experimentation and feedback – without having had those experiences it can feel, to the NT partner, like kissing a 15-year-old who has absolutely no idea what to do.

Sex seems only to work for Chris in certain positions. This is a lack of physical and emotional synchrony, almost as though, if you have a procedure, a way that things work, why change the procedure? Variety is not the spice of life. Sensory sensitivity is common, and there can also be a lack of awareness that intimacy is more important in a relationship than just for conception.

Rachel then comments that *'although he is an engineer and an artist and can do really intricate work with his hands, he struggles to give a massage that is not repetitive and clumsy'*. What is required here is for Chris to actually switch off his frontal lobe and work with his heart. For a person with Asperger's syndrome this is very difficult to do and is one of the reasons emotional intimacy with another person is such a challenge for them.

Rachel says *'I have found that sex is often the only way Chris can express his love'*. Yes – and there can almost be a belief that sex measures the quality of the relationship. There may be repetitive sex, routine sex or sex that is always at a particular time, on a particular day or occasion – for example, every day when you wake up in the morning. To the NT partner, this can feel as though you are no longer making love but that you are being used as a form of masturbation. So there can be major issues here where the couple need a lot of specific and specialist support.

Rachel says:

> I will often ask Chris how he is feeling, on a scale of 1 to 10, where 1 is suicidal and 10 is the happiest possible. It's so funny how, from his behaviour, I'd have said he felt maybe a 2, and he says 'eight'!

Yes, I understand this. The face, and sometimes the body language and tone of voice of a person with AS, will not necessarily give you any insight into how the person is feeling. In fact it can almost seem as though a mask goes on and you then find, and are surprised, that the person may be happier than their still face would suggest.

Chris comments that Rachel *'has to have a finely balanced combination of positive emotion and physical wellbeing to be intimate'*.

That's right, but that may not be the AS way. Sex is an act, not necessarily one that requires you to be in an emotionally good frame of mind or have a sense of wellbeing and a feeling of love. We use the phrase 'making love' and a person with Asperger's syndrome may not be good at creating that – other than what they've seen in the movies. As a result of not having had many romantic relationships during adolescence, the AS partner may have little understanding about aspects of sexuality. Their source of information may have been, and may still be, pornography and the belief that pornography equals intimacy. There also can be less appreciation of the conventional boundaries in areas of sexuality. This may include sadomasochism, cross-dressing and a whole range of areas in which the person maybe far more open to experimentation than their NT partner feels comfortable with. So it is possible that issues can arise where AS partners may have explored aspects of sexuality via pornography and want to experience what that is like within the relationship, without recognizing that the NT partner may not wish to go in that particular direction.

Chris says *'intimacy helps me feel better. I find it relieves stress, aids sleep and rest, lifts mood and eases worries.'* So, for Chris, sex has a functional purpose, it makes him feel better. It is not necessarily an interpersonal expression of the relationship. People might say, 'Oh, that's a male behaviour'. Well, that may be the case to some extent, but this is really taken to an extreme – and that is the problem. Because none of the characteristics of ASC are unique – they all exist in the ordinary population, but it is the intensity of them and the pattern that creates the relationship problem.

Chris uses a lovely phrase here: *'I think the main difference between the two of us is that intimacy for me is the cause of wellbeing, whereas with Rachel it comes very much more as a result of wellbeing.'* I think this is very perceptive. This is where, when intimacy issues are becoming a problem, the couple need relationship counselling from a counsellor specializing in areas of sexuality within a relationship.

Why do people with Asperger's syndrome find emotional intimacy with another human being so hard?

One of the most important diagnostic criteria for ASC is an impairment in social and emotional reciprocity. One of the first things we look at diagnostically is the ability not only to be reciprocal but also to make a connection with someone. This difficult connecting is due to a different neurology. The areas of the brain that facilitate this ability do not work effectively in the AS brain.

Why does it seem that many people with Asperger's syndrome become obsessive or extreme over people and things? There seems to be an inability to moderate – it's all or nothing.
Yes. There seems to be an issue in ASC of intensity. It is either hardly ever or it is too intense, and both extremes can be very difficult to cope with. Moderating is very difficult for a person with Asperger's syndrome.

In terms of the early stages of a relationship, the NT partner often becomes the 'special interest' and is pursued with a level of intensity that can, initially anyway, be perceived to be extremely flattering. It may not be what you have experienced in other relationships, and it is easy to believe that this will be a lifelong experience when, in reality, it is only temporary. Adjusting to the reality can be very upsetting because you feel you have known that your AS partner has the ability to behave differently and is now, apparently, choosing not to do so. This can feel like rejection and be very hurtful to the NT partner.

The special interest gives the AS partner enjoyment. It's a thought blocker, giving them energy – but each interest has a 'use by' date – and that can include the relationship.

How does the AS/NT relationship make physical and emotional intimacy work?
This is an area that needs to be worked at, taking time, commitment, understanding of each other and compromise from both partners. In a way, emotional intimacy is the ultimate area of challenge for a person with Asperger's syndrome, and it really goes to the basics of the characteristics of Asperger's syndrome. It is the ultimate and most elusive goal. Physical and emotional intimacy can be built up by discussion between partners around the following questions:

- How difficult or easy is it for you to talk about your inner thoughts and feelings with your partner?

- Are there any strategies you have discovered that help you to share your inner thoughts and feelings?

- What constitutes emotional intimacy for you?

- How do you know when your partner wants emotional intimacy?

- Are your physical intimacy needs for *affection* currently fulfilled (percentage figure)?

- Are your *sex* needs currently fulfilled (percentage figure)?

- What's preventing that fulfilment? Issues might relate to:

  — opportunity

  — privacy

  — energy

  — performance expectations

  — sexual confidence and knowledge

  — sexual information and preferences

  — feeling sexually attractive

  — sensory sensitivity

  — sexual frequency

  — sexual satisfaction for self and partner.

Rachel and Chris talk about 'false messages'. How common is it for an NT partner to misread their partner's signals and how can we improve this? This is a common problem as the AS partner often lacks the vocabulary to describe their emotional state. Using the method, as Rachel and Chris are doing, of numbers on a scale of 1 to 10 (where 1 is very sad and 10 is ecstatic), it is much easier for the AS partner to identify how they are feeling. They can respond with a number far more easily than having to try and put into words how they are feeling. If someone has Asperger's syndrome and is also pedantic, you might get the answer 'I'm an 8.25'!

One of the problems within the area of intimacy in a neurodiverse relationship is that the amount of knowledge the AS partner has is either zero or too much. Zero, because they've never had a relationship and so it is very much new territory – 'I don't like it, I feel uncomfortable and I'm not sure if I am any good.' Or, they have a lot of information, not gained from relationships but from sources such as pornography that may give them a false expectation of what a partner wants and what they should do.

Does drinking alcohol or smoking dope have any benefits in reducing anxiety and inhibitions in this area – as it might to an NT person?
Alcohol is a relaxant and so, if the AS person is having intimacy performance anxiety, drinking might suppress the anxiety. However, the issue here for someone with Asperger's syndrome is one of moderation. So what can happen is the person can quickly become intoxicated when drinking alcohol. The level of alcohol needed to give a sense of relaxation is surpassed and that person may now be drunk – and having sex with a drunk is not a good idea!

The same would apply to marijuana. People take it to be 'out of it' and to relax, but in intimacy you want to be 'in it' not 'out of it'! So, in other words, there is a barrier of intoxication either by alcohol or drugs which is not good. From my clinical experience, the level of AS alcoholics and those with drug problems is disproportionately high.

The latest research suggests that one in four of the clients of alcohol and drug dependency services have signs of Asperger's syndrome. One in four – that is a high percentage. Yes, drinking 'takes the edge off it'. But people with AS need their frontal lobes to process social information in order to work out what to say and do. Unable to do this intuitively, they must do it cognitively – but the frontal lobes are soluble in alcohol. So, once the person starts drinking alcohol, the cognitive control of AS characteristics dissolves and they become AS uninhibited – and that's not good.

10

Meltdowns

NEIL'S STORY

We all sense the build-up: the shoulders move up, there's continual frowning at everything and everyone, even while asleep. The stimming (self-stimulation) becomes more obvious, intense and frequent. Conversation deteriorates as sarcasm and criticism colour any remarks and responses. As the tension builds, I notice myself tingling all over, with my own mounting anticipation and frustration, worsened by my inability to rest or sleep. I dare not speak lest I provoke the eruption that I know must come. The issue now is what or who will trigger the detonation – and it can be the tiniest thing.

Once upon a time I found myself pushed into meltdown by sensing that people were withdrawing from me, further limiting the little communication I already received. My meltdown was simply an attempt to elicit some, any, response. Did it make an impression? Did it ever resolve an issue? Was I heard, even then? The reality is that all the energy invested in a meltdown is wasted, since the result, commonly, is that people withdraw further. The perpetrator is left unaddressed and unlikely to be revisited since the experience was too unpleasant. Over time you get an overwhelming sense of futility and exhaustion from neurotypical (NT) people. 'Why doesn't he get it? Why isn't he like other people who can express their feelings rationally rather than bottling up the anger and then exploding?' You notice that, for the NT partner, a major issue develops and worsens over time because they may be the only person who witnesses the meltdowns. Others, with a more casual interaction with the AS individual, often find it hard to accept that meltdowns even occur, wondering whether the partner is the problem. This only serves to increase the damage. This is known as the Cassandra syndrome.

Meltdowns may be especially hard to deal with for those not prepared for the event, who may find it quite atypical of a person they have perceived to be generally quiet, competent and meticulous in their work.

Five years ago a junior colleague confessed that he was scared of me. He worked for a related division but not under my direct responsibility. We had always seemed to get on well and I respected his ability. I had never taken him to task and had helped with his instruction. Why was he scared of me? This year I realized why. In our sometimes very demanding environment he had witnessed a meltdown. Dr Banner had become the Incredible Hulk and the transformation left him uncertain... what about next time?

If your job puts you in the company of those who are also prone to meltdowns, the place can resemble a war zone at times, with random detonations occurring everywhere. Worse still will be the situation for the NT partner in a family in which, not only does her partner have AS issues, but the children as well. To outsiders, the family may seem 'ideal'. However, on the inside there is a perpetual lurching from episode to episode, depending on the distribution of stress. Although everyone suffers, the NT partner suffers the most.

Then the diagnosis is suggested, and confirmed, and you realize you can't change the wiring. However, you might be able to modify the effects of the circuitry to avert disaster. I now at least understand what's happening from the frame of reference of AS. Often (now) I even know why I'm reacting the way I am and am learning to anticipate an episode. Here's what I've learned about meltdowns through my own experiences:

The setting: There is often a victim or target. This person is often not the original source of frustration and mounting anxiety which have led to the reaction. Alternatively, an individual or group has recurrently niggled or repeatedly failed to achieve expected goals. My most illustrative analogy is the activation energy diagram for an exothermic reaction: not much happens for a while as the fuse (which might be short or long) is burning, then... *bang!*... followed by intense quiet. No one dares comment lest they provoke another episode – they don't appreciate that the energy has already dissipated.

What it feels like to have a meltdown: Your head's about to explode, though it's pressure, not pain. There's intense frustration and anger and wanting to strike out at the perceived perpetrator verbally or (sometimes) physically. Initially there is muscular tension, which progresses through gross tremor to a level where fine motor skills are impossible. Your sense of the consequences of words and actions rapidly diminishes, with a loss of social and situational awareness. There's an intense focus on the event, which seems to be escaping your control, and on punishing the apparent perpetrator(s) regardless of how aware they actually are of the issue. It's an almost overwhelming sense that *'You should know this'* (as though they should read your expectations). And a sense of intense distress that everyone else fails to appreciate the importance of the event – you are the only one who knows or cares.

What it looks like to everyone else: The 'exploder' may initially seem tense, then abrupt, then hyperactive. He (since this is a male-dominated event) will be breathing more rapidly and deeply and appear to be less attentive to external cues, particularly verbal (hence why, after a while, he doesn't hear external attempts to placate him). His vision may be targeted and focused or he might be casting around, seemingly searching for a target for his mounting rage (a good time to duck or don an invisibility cloak). This may be accompanied by an impressive level of facial flushing.

What it sounds like: The meltdown begins with increasingly monotonic monologue through increasingly clenched teeth. There's a progressive increase in volume, directness and sometimes pitch, along with a loss of social appropriateness (expect some original combinations of standard language mixed with novel deprecatory comparisons).

What 'drives' it: Physiologically, this is a classic 'fight/flight' reaction, so cardiac output and muscular efforts increase ('super-human' strength). Imagine pouring increasing amounts of adrenaline into a system that is already exporting maximum motor-neuronal output. For the person having the meltdown there is a loss of control.

The aftermath: After the climax there's sheer exhaustion – both mental and physical. You feel intense shame and regret, but the anger usually persists: 'You pushed me too far, again. You deserved this; why didn't you just do as I asked, as any rational, responsible person would?' Then you forget it, as if it never happened: 'No bad feelings, just do it right next time, OK?' Except it's not that easy. The NT partner may react back: '*You* have a communication problem!' The word *you* often comes like a finger poking into your chest. Or, '*You* need anger management classes' (not *I* or *we* need to clean up *our* act). The reality is that you often cannot withdraw (well, I can't anyway). The task can't be simply left or postponed. You proceed through the awkward silence, you hear the faint sound of people around you walking on eggshells. Then comes regret, self-deprecation and ever-worsening depression. 'Where does this ogre come from? How can I keep him caged?'

What it achieves: Usually nothing, unless the witnesses are strongly motivated (out of fear) to change things to avoid a repeat. The preferred change is to get rid of the perpetrator (the AS partner) rather than fix the system. As the person who has had the meltdown, even if you're right, you might end up out.

Symptoms and signs of danger: Not being able to complete or assign priority to a task due to being interrupted or required to perform in some other way. Be aware of bristling, grunting assent or curt responses, accompanied by restlessness, inability to focus and an unwillingness to embark on any activity.

What feeds the meltdown: Much of the time, people with an ASC can be their own worst enemies in laying the foundations for a meltdown. Physical tiredness, sleep deprivation, ignoring the cold until you shiver, which raises adrenaline levels, hunger (same mechanism), alcohol and other dis-inhibitory influences all contribute. Other triggers may be poor time-management (being in a rush), task overload (often self-inflicted), perceived (and feared) consequences of failing to meet deadlines and perceptions of external inflexibility, along with an inability to negotiate a compromise. Other sparks can be excessive and unrealistic expectations of self and others, fear of losing face, failure to achieve a desired outcome in a reasonable time or anxiety about not being in control (especially in a situation which resulted in a previous meltdown).

Antidepressants and mood stabilizers can make anxiety symptoms worse. You become increasingly twitchy but the tablets can mask the reasons why. Oblivious to the warning signs, huge meltdowns can erupt without warning. The volcano moves underwater!

What minimizes the episode: Planning, consultation and communicating needs and priorities – either to the individual or by the individual. Permission and help, from the perspective of the AS partner, for them to focus on achieving the best possible outcome.

What minimizes the damage: Being able to escape, nicotine spray (works for some people), surviving and dealing with the consequences, *doing better next time*.

What else can happen: Shutting down is a less obvious but probably far more dangerous reaction to overload in the person with the ASC. It's a failure or inability to resolve the episode, causing withdrawal. It presents a bit like fainting in front of a predator rather than running away. The predator may choose not to eat you, but it becomes impossible for the person to get up without being eaten!

Two years ago my boss was discussing with me a report from a trainee of one of my 'episodes' of extreme impatience, and how out-of-character it was. I too, was personally disturbed and stated that, since being on mood stabilizers, I had lost any sense of when these reactions were about to occur. I said that I hated them, along with my inability to detect or control them and slowly weaned myself off the medication, hoping to regain some control. I seriously doubt that anyone has ever enjoyed having a meltdown.

When a toddler believes he deserves something or wants something to happen, it doesn't occur to him that things might be inconvenient, inappropriate or unfeasible. He wants it, now, and if he doesn't get it, everyone is going to know how unreasonable *you* are by denying him it. So he throws a tantrum. He neither

NEURODIVERSE RELATIONSHIPS

recognizes nor cares that this type of behaviour makes people cringe rather than ally themselves with him. He has little sense of how he is perceived. For a person with AS, the difference lies in the lack of a focused objective for their 'tantrum'. The emotional overload, without discernible relief, wreaks havoc in a brain that, typically, needs to put all events into context in a timely manner.

In reality, for the person with the ASC, few people notice you unless they want something or you do something exceptional. Meltdowns can be pretty exceptional, but in the wrong way. You are not going to get what you want (willingly), and others are not going to respect you or your wishes as a result.

ANNIE'S STORY

Our task is to discuss the accursed manifestation of autistic spectrum conditions – the meltdown, aka the 'big bang' phenomenon or having a Fukushima. As well as writing about how meltdowns affect us personally, we're going to talk about the theories and facts behind them.

The 'meltdown' is commonly considered a characteristic of individuals on the autistic spectrum, it being particularly evident as a maladaptive behavioural aspect of Asperger-type individuals. It may well be the most obvious sign to others that 'this guy ain't quite right' even though he appears 'normal' in other areas. It can be the most troublesome problem to deal with, as meltdowns serve to alienate people with whom the AS individual may need to interact, such as partners, family, friends, work colleagues, supervisors and therapists. These events can result in a 'glass ceiling' effect being applied to the individual; he or she may be deemed too risky to be entrusted with critical tasks for which they might otherwise be thought suitable or desirable. Similarly, the person may self-limit their own advancement as they develop anxiety about poorly timed outbursts, particularly as they may have little or no warning of an episode. I would suggest that a meltdown is the AS equivalent of a seizure in an individual affected by epilepsy: there often appears to be no systematic initiating cause, and the effect can be beyond voluntary control. One major difference is the way in which the event is received. Sympathy and reassurance are rarely offered to the perpetrator of a meltdown. Meltdowns can also be self-perpetuating: anxiety over the possibility of an unanticipated emotional outburst increases the likelihood of it happening.

Since even high-functioning AS people limit their communication, the more pervasive manifestations of AS can easily go undetected for long periods of time. Unsurprisingly, it is communication issues that will often instigate a meltdown, as a person with AS will often interpret information too literally, incompletely or incorrectly. It would be unwise to perpetrate a practical joke on an AS person.

The underlying cause of a meltdown may come from two sources: a situation arises in which there is no understanding of, or scant regard for, the expectations of the AS individual; and simultaneously, the AS individual is unaware that he is becoming emotionally 'loaded'. Indeed, emotional tension may have been building up over the preceding hours or days and the 'straw that breaks the camel's back' becomes the trigger. Once the weapon is fired, it is impossible to restrain the reaction until its energy is dispersed. The unwitting 'victim' has dealt the last straw and is left (justifiably) bewildered by the situation.

This unpleasant phenomenon becomes a persistent source of anxiety to both the person with AS and their associates. The closer the association, the more likely this maladaptive behaviour will have been witnessed and that the family member, friend or colleague will have been the apparent target of the meltdown. Often the worst affected are family. Parents of an AS child having a meltdown would have got used to them and have developed 'strategies' to deal with the situation. These strategies may not be useful or transferable and may have served to reinforce the meltdown. Approaches such as 'He's always had a short fuse', 'He gets easily upset at apparently trivial things' or 'We tend to ignore it, ride it out and then everything settles down' don't provide any insight to the AS individual. Nor do they help the individual to modify their circumstances and responses in order to minimize or avert further episodes. It's worth noting that the occupants of Pompeii ignored Mount Vesuvius's minor eruptions to their ultimate peril. If the AS individual has a partner and children, the situation will be decidedly more complex and difficult.

Tony Attwood's
Commentary and Q&A

Annie gives the analogy of meltdowns being similar to epilepsy. They certainly can be in the sense that, like an epileptic seizure, once a meltdown has begun it is incredibly difficult for either the person to whom it is happening or the people around them to stop it. There are warning signs, but they may not be easy to spot and, although a meltdown may appear to come out of the blue, it will, in fact, have been building up over time.

It is common that meltdowns are not seen within the initial stages of the relationship or courtship. So the AS person has been able to cognitively control themselves and not allow you to see 'the dark side'. It is, on the one hand, encouraging that the person can do that, albeit for a limited time, but, on the other hand, disappointing to know that it is too much to expect that same effort for ever more.

Often the person with Asperger's syndrome is the last to be aware that the meltdown is on its way. It's almost as though the frontal lobes are not getting the information. I ask NT partners to draw a thermometer with a list of the early warning signs of a meltdown in terms of behaviour, language, thinking, actions and circumstances at various points on the thermometer. There are often telltale signs that one is on the way – and prevention is better than cure. It may mean then bringing the early warning signs to the attention of the AS partner. For example, by saying 'On the thermometer of zero to ten you are at six and rising. We need to work on this before you reach seven – which is the point of no return.' Sometimes, being aware of their anger is something the person with Asperger's syndrome will want to hide from their partner, but they can find this very hard to do.

It is terrifying for children in the relationship because they will see their parent behaving like a toddler – but with the size and ferocity of an adult. The metaphor of an epileptic seizure is quite appropriate, because you just can't get through to the person and, when children feel that they can't get through and are not being heard, that's very frightening for them.

175

Meltdowns seem to be a constitutional part of AS. However, the AS person, throughout childhood, may have learned that throwing a wobbly means that you get what you want. This learned behaviour can subsequently be used as manipulation. With an NT fearing the anger attack, they will do anything to prevent it. The threat of a meltdown can be used by the AS partner to deliberately manipulate situations. Sometimes the meltdown is due to a build-up of being overwhelmed by social, conversational, sensory and cognitive aspects. There is a build-up of tension that is released in the meltdown – but then the AS partner can start to use that as emotional blackmail. We are used to the term 'international terrorism'; I call this 'domestic terrorism' – it achieves control in the family environment. Controlling by fear is basically bullying – which is ironic, because the person with Asperger's syndrome has often been the focus of bullies at school.

Why do meltdowns occur? How would you know if the meltdown was intentional?
The difference is in the eyes. In a genuine meltdown there is a look of absolute panic and despair: 'I have to get out of here, I am overwhelmed.' That's versus a glint in the eye and a feeling that this is under cognitive control in an intended meltdown. It is hard to define, but sometimes you know by the circumstances if the meltdown is a bid to control. A meltdown *is* a constitutional part of Asperger's syndrome, but that does not always mean it is out of the person's control.

Neil says: *'Your sense of the consequences of words and actions rapidly diminishes, with a loss of social and situational awareness. There's an intense focus on the event, which seems to be escaping your control.'* That is the issue – the lack of control. Then there's the punishment of the apparent perpetrator, 'You must be punished for doing something wrong.' This 'punishment' will affect both the partner and the children of the person with AS. Quite often the AS parent is a strict disciplinarian and expects obedience and learning by fear rather than by compassion, understanding and explanation. Neil's comment *'punishment of the apparent perpetrator'* is ominous. In other words, his satisfactory resolution and closure is retribution and punishment. This is where the NT partner has to adjust their management strategies in various situations according to the developmental level of their partner, which may range from two-year-old temper tantrums to adolescence, despite the fact that, intellectually, their partner may be superior to others. The NT parent will also be thinking about the children and the issues that the meltdown may cause there.

Another reason that meltdowns occur is not so much as a reaction to a situation as a build-up of tension – various things occur and you have an explosion to cleanse the system. It is almost like you will only feel better when you have vomited and cleared the system. This is a way of rebooting the emotion computer. So after this intense explosion the Aspie says, 'I'm OK now', but the partner says, 'It's going to take me days to get over what you just said and did.' The Aspie may respond with 'Now I'm fine. You should be happy I'm OK. Why are you crying? What's the problem?' Unfortunately, the person with AS often has this instantaneous intense reaction, but it ends so quickly that it can be what psychologists call negative reinforcement. It is like paracetamol to a headache. So if they've had a bad day at work and they're feeling tense, they have this explosion of emotions and then they're OK. But for all of those around them, it's hell.

What is happening psychologically when someone is having a meltdown?
It is essentially going beyond the point of no return. I like Annie's analogy of a seizure during epilepsy. What is happening is an intense explosion of energy that nobody can control.

Annie states that certain strategies from NT friends and family may make meltdowns worse rather than help the AS individual modify their circumstances and responses. What responses from NT friends and family would help the AS person?
The family needs a script or a 'safety plan' for when a meltdown occurs. It may include the NT partner saying, 'I'll deal with this', and the kids go to their rooms.

What is your advice for NT people experiencing an AS meltdown? Should they step in and try to reason with the person or let it run its course?
Don't forget that you (the NT partner) are emotionally agitated yourself, emotional in all senses. But don't get angry, as that will just serve to add fuel to the fire. Don't get sad and despondent, that will

do the same. Don't use affection. How you deal with it is the same way that you might deal with problems on a journey. For example, today I typed a postcode into the GPS and it told me 'at Junction.10, take the fourth exit. Technically, it was the fifth, but I took the fourth. Now, had I had an AS partner sitting beside me and I had followed the wrong road, they might say 'What are you doing? We're going to be late!' and have had a huge explosion about it. But the GPS recalculates and calmly asks me to make a legal U-turn. It makes no mention of my error. So the partner needs to be that GPS – to focus on what to do in a calm way. The GPS did not say 'Tony, I said the fourth exit and you have gone down the wrong one, were you listening to me?' It doesn't criticize, it doesn't highlight what I did wrong, and it calmly tells me how to repair the situation. So in the safety plan for a meltdown, these are things that must be considered. The next strategy is don't ask, 'What's your problem? What are you upset about?' The person having the meltdown is in a state of emotional distress and they want to move out of it – not recall how they got into it. Eloquence in describing thoughts is elusive to them in a meltdown and they cannot explain it, they just want to get out of that situation.

Could the NT partner just get out of there and leave them to it?
That's the next part of the sequence. We've got to look now at the AS partner's off switch. The off switch may be solitary tranquility, staying away from people and finding somewhere (even if it is the toilet!) to get away from other people and to be alone. But sometimes the off switch is the special interest. So you may say, 'I think it would be a good idea if you played your favourite game on your computer or looked through your collection of photographs of World War II tanks. When you're looking at your photographs of tanks you feel happy, you enjoy it, it's fun and you know so much.' So the off switch might be solitude, the special interest or sometimes being outside, surrounded by nature. It is the thought blocker antidote to the emotional and sensory overload the person with AS is experiencing.

Finally, after the event when the person is calm, you could suggest, 'We need to learn from this. What was happening and how we can prevent it in the future?' However, if you ask this too early on, you are not going to get a sensible answer and may even inflame the situation. You've got to choose your time carefully to debrief. If you get the timing right and are able to do this, the first thing to go through is the AS partner's perspective, then go through your own and (if applicable) the perspective of the children in the family. Explain to them, 'We have a problem here that needs to be resolved.'

How can AS/NT partners work together to minimize the frequency and damage caused by meltdowns?
What you're trying to do is encourage self-awareness. You want your AS partner to say, 'I'm feeling a bit irritated – on my thermometer I have just passed five,' but that requires conscious insight. One strategy that costs a bit financially but is really useful is sports technology such as a heart rate monitor. This can be set as an alarm, and when the Aspie's heart rate gets to 135 or 140, the alarm goes off. If you want a measure that someone can use to monitor their level of anxiety and irritation, these can be useful. For example, it will tell your heart rate throughout the day – this can be very helpful in identifying situations associated with stress and anxiety and can become a cue to indicate the need for stress-reduction strategies. These devices can continuously record heart rate throughout the day, and on returning from work the NT partner can then sit down with the AS partner and go through the day's stresses in order to minimize the risk of meltdowns at home.

11

Parenting

TRISHA'S STORY

I have known my husband Max since I was 12 years old. We were married when I was 19 and Max was 21. Max comes from an Italian family and I come from an Australian one – it was just my mother and me. So our backgrounds are worlds apart. Max is the actor-type Aspie. He blends into any person or culture, mimicking everything from gestures to accents. He was always the comedian, putting on a performance wherever we went. I was quiet and better with one-on-one situations.

Our daughter was born in the first year we were married. It was a difficult birth followed by a bout of post-natal depression. I had assumed Max's change in personality was due to us having a baby and the increased financial stress. Max no longer communicated with me or acknowledged my depression. The first 12 years of our daughter's life was primarily left to me – although Max did help with our daughter's bath and bed routine at night. He loved the early years of playing with her, as if he was a big brother. From a young age though, our daughter suffered severe learning disabilities and undiagnosed Asperger's syndrome with severe anxiety. As she grew up, it became very hard for Max to cope with her.

During those early years, Max's obsession was work and study. This was his first priority, our daughter was second and I was there to do everything else. It was to the point of me being put on the shelf as he regularly gave priority to deadlines, assignments or projects. When he was sent away for work for six weeks, he returned as though the previous ten years had disappeared. It felt as though all our history had gone and we had to start from the beginning. Never growing up or moving forward together, we lived in separate worlds, and I was here for the Max ride. He was unaware of my hopes, dreams, aspirations or needs – they were not there for him to participate in. Where was my comedian and friend you may ask? This side of Max came out only at work or in social situations. As soon as we came home, another Max would come out. This led to despair and loneliness for me. I would ask why, I would ask Max to tell me how he felt, but this would be met with silence and withdrawal. I could see he had very little to give to me and our daughter. He lacked the ability to be there day-to-day, although he was great in crises.

So I set about making the best out of the situation and being the best mum I could be for our daughter. I studied and worked around her schedule of dance, music, speech and therapies. I was at every school function and dance practice and recital. I filled my life with our daughter and I had a very close relationship with her.

Things changed during our daughter's puberty for Max and me. Our daughter changed physically early on and became emotional, depressed and anxiety-riddled. As her needs and anxiety increased, Max disconnected from her. He had empathy to a point, but this could quickly turn to indifference. I would have to work harder at comforting our daughter. I had also just fallen pregnant with our son. At the same time, Max's career was on the move. He had started work in construction, which meant moving from project to project. I inconveniently developed ante-natal psychosis and post-natal psychosis during that pregnancy, which continued after our son's birth.

Four house moves later, our daughter had reached the 'terrible teens' and by the age of 15 had developed mental health issues. Max was away a lot, and during this time our son regressed into autism. When he was at home, Max would help with all the housework and get up to see our son, but he was not there emotionally for either me or our daughter because it was too overwhelming and confusing for him. His anxiety increased and he would shut down more and more. Max hid happily in his familiar work routine while home was a mess. Personally, I was trying to survive one day at a time, mourning my son's autism and comforting my rebellious teenager – and doing it all alone.

At that breaking point, I sought counselling for myself and my daughter. I put my son into early intervention and threw myself into learning all I could about autism. I asked Max to come to counselling and learn about autism too, but he refused to be a part of it. My son, my daughter and I had improved significantly but

Max continued to decline, working himself into hospital and never able to open up about his feelings. At 18 years old our daughter was finally diagnosed with Asperger's syndrome and mental health issues. A while later, Max had a breakdown and asked for help as he felt suicidal. He went to a psychiatrist and was diagnosed with depression and anxiety disorder. Slowly, with time, Max got better and started communicating and processing. He was able to put strategies in place and started to assemble scripts for coping. After 20 years I felt I was getting to know the real Max and our relationship started to grow. We were now communicating and, if he needed time to process, I respected that.

When our daughter was 23 and had finished her studies, she joined the work force and left home to get married. On that day she essentially cut all her family and friends off. This broke my heart and, in the years since, I fell to pieces. This was the first time Max had seen and felt the effects of being put on the shelf and replaced. At that point, Max said he would not put us on the shelf again although it takes a toll on him. I see he needs a lot of alone time and that it is very important that he gets his time to go for an early run or to the gym.

We have now reached 26 years of marriage and our son is now a teenager. He is in full puberty and has essentially switched to wanting Max only. He craves his dad's attention and time. He only comes to me if he is sick or Max cannot understand what he needs. It is still tough for Max, although our son is nothing like our daughter. I would consider him easier, though Max has said to me that both children are taxing for him.

I can see we both have different approaches to raising our children. Max was great with physical care, playing with them when they were young and generous with money. As things got more intense with our daughter, he disconnected permanently and was not able to reconnect with her again. Now, with our son, he doesn't feel the pull to disconnect in the same way. We both realize he is the best role model to show our son how to be an ASC man. Max communicates with him better than he does with me. They speak the same language. I realize, due to my daughter not being diagnosed early and the limited information available about female Aspies, that I was trying to raise her to be an NT person – a role she could not fit. I was too emotional. She grew up under pressure and instability. We are raising our son very differently. He is benefiting from a peaceful, mature marriage, from a dad that does not disconnect and who 'gets him'. Max is teaching him some of his actor techniques and social training to cope with life. I have learned you can't change an Aspie. You can only set the boundaries and not let yourself be consumed by autism and AS. I used to sacrifice myself for everyone else's needs. I hope I am more balanced now in looking after myself. I am so happy to be where we are today – it was worth the journey.

MAX'S STORY

I wanted to be different, so universally unlike the 'traditional' Italian family that I grew up in, and Trisha was it! I was 14 years old when I first saw her. She was a very giving, outspoken, free-spirited and vivacious girl who represented the complete opposite of my home life. Years later, when we dated, she did not make it easy for me; I had to ask her seven times to marry me. I pulled out every script I had, polished my façade and chased her down so that eventually she said yes. We were married very young and, once the wedding day was done, I changed completely. So quickly that it was literally overnight – the script was finished, the façade had served its purpose, Trisha was now just along for the ride.

Trisha fell pregnant four weeks into our marriage, and when our daughter was born I felt love, fear and anxiety all at the same time. I found myself realizing that I was not ready to become a dad at 21.

I was a divided father during our daughter's early years. I was so preoccupied with work and study that I found any unrelated interruption, including illness, to be intolerable – an unwelcome intruder to my schedule. I would come home from work ready to enjoy all the 'soft stuff', bathing our daughter, feeding time, bedtime stories – each and every night – it was an easy routine. I seriously thought I was the greatest dad. I left all the emotional 'heavy lifting' to Trisha without giving consideration to her depressed and suffering mental state. I put everything on her and, unless she initiated anything, I made no reasonable attempt to move forward or change.

As our daughter started to attend school, her learning disabilities and AS (undiagnosed at this time) became more pronounced. This became a point of frustration on my part. Since I always did well at school, it was almost unforgivable. I tried to teach her maths (being an engineer) and this only led to a great deal of misery on our daughter's part. The frustration, anger and arguments between Trisha and me increased, mostly due to my inability to approach a task from more than one direction. I was not easily able to communicate at the same level as either my five-year-old daughter or my 20-something-year-old wife!

Arguments with Trisha were many and varied but had a common theme that centred around my focus with work and my lack of attention and connection at home. This was referred to as the 'teaspoon' of support that, as a father or husband, I gave to fill Trisha's 'emotional bucket'. I found that during these times, the hardest questions Trisha would ask of me would be 'Why did you do that?' and 'What are you feeling?' 'Why?' I gave her blank stares. I shut down – mixed it up with anxiety and self-loathing for not doing better (i.e. 'Why can't I just get it right?'). Many times I felt that I was on the edge of a precipice and the answer to the 'why?' lay on a ledge on the other side of a bottomless chasm. I could 'sense' a required answer but was not able to bridge the gap with any words – there was a lot of silence. I could only do the next best thing – clean the house. I would leave these issues unresolved not just for the night or next day, but for the weeks that followed. This was my routine for the first half of our married life. For over ten years we repeated the same scenario.

Our daughter reached puberty, a change that led to a significant readjustment in my mind. As if on cue, I retired my role as dad. I never thought of an expiry date, but there it was – her physical and emotional growth meant that, like her mum, she could be put on the shelf – 'job done!' Our son was born when our daughter was 12 years old – so I replayed the same routine all over again.

During our daughter's early teen years, Trisha was more perceptive than I was. She would regularly bring to my attention the need to protect our daughter from herself, her poor judgement, teenage boys who would take advantage of her, social media and the internet. In this area of parenting I took my cues from Trisha. We worked well together. I became a 'crisis dad' – turning up to school, talking to the Principal and teachers, addressing aggrieved parents, sorting out teenage boys, etc. I became good at fixing the problem once I was made aware of the problem. I could not foresee or perceive it – I was totally clueless. However, I can look back and be proud of this singular fact, that: As parents, we never ever took it out on each other or blamed each other. I may have been vacant – but I was never malicious, something we came to realize when we started going to the Queensland Asperger Partners Support Group QAPS workshops, run by Tony Attwood.

I am content in the knowledge that I can see times where our daughter would come to me first to disclose anything she knew that would upset us both. I guess I was a soft target, since my initial reaction was always fact-based and not emotional, unlike Trisha. We differed greatly in this area in the initial part of every matter raised. I needed a longer processing time to collect my thoughts and would then relate the matter to Trisha to verify the issue and keep up. In this way we would deal with it together – with Trisha taking the lead.

Our daughter finished her schooling and started work. I became more intolerant of her dependency, both emotionally and financially. When she was 20, I thought she was old enough to earn her keep and move on. My view was, 'I did it, so why can't she?' I failed to take into account her developmental age and AS traits. This was a point of contention between Trisha and me. I believed that there was very little time left from Trisha for either our son or me and that Trisha had become consumed with helping our daughter (which was always our daughter's goal).

Our son's diagnosis of autism at the age of two took a heavy toll on the family. Trisha and our daughter sought help through counselling, but I immersed myself in the safe routine of work; so much so that I was working myself into an early grave (being hospitalized twice). Eventually I became disturbed, deeply depressed and anxious to the point of contemplating self-harm. I finally listened to Trisha and went to counselling – it was the best thing I ever did.

I found it very hard to communicate with my daughter throughout her life – and I struggle with this even now. But since I attended counselling I have found the ability *and the desire* to communicate more openly with both my wife and my son. I am more mindful and present in the moment, which allows me to be involved. It is exhausting, but rewarding at the same time. I need more down time. Our daughter is married and has left home but, in doing so, has also cut off her family. I witnessed firsthand the effects that AS can have on a relationship, especially between a mother and daughter (who were very close – to the point of obsession, which reminded me of my own early obsession with Trisha). Our daughter has put my wife on the shelf now, and it has broken Trisha's heart. This experience brought out the 'crisis husband', and since our daughter's departure I have remained connected to my wife and our son.

Out of necessity I have had to create new pathways (scripts and switches) for communication, changes in routine and focus. Progressively, my perception and processing time has gone from three weeks to the same day. I can sense when Trisha or our son are not themselves or are ill and can now act with a measure of tolerance (still working on empathy). My son is 12 years old and going through puberty now and, just like with my daughter, I have the urge to say, 'There, job done!' and retire the dad role. But two things prevent me from doing this:

- realizing he needs me, and

- he won't let me retire and shelve him!

As an AS dad I can do many things for my son, mostly centred on work, which I can relate to and identify with since they are areas which I can control. It takes a determined effort to make and keep a change – to include and trust someone profoundly. Trisha had to wait 21 years for me to acknowledge and believe this fact. I have made a determined effort to build on my experience with our daughter and make a change to contribute to our son's life.

I have come to love and appreciate Trisha more over these last five years together, and I do it without a script or façade. We have gone from strength to strength and are now resilient and content. Her laughter is what makes me happy now.

I have had to ask, 'What's in it for me?' I am here because of my own choosing – I chose my wife – this is my life, I need to own it by being responsible to those nearest to me.

Tony Attwood's Commentary and Q&A

In this chapter, Max talks openly about pursuing Trisha in order to marry her. '*I...chased her down so that eventually she said yes.*' The AS partner will often show persistence and perseverance until they have what they want. Max goes on... '*once the wedding day was done, I changed completely. So quickly that it was literally overnight.*' This is common too – and it is interesting that Max recognizes his behaviour. That's it, he's got the prize (Trisha) and he doesn't need to try any more.

Trisha says, '*I see he needs a lot of alone time*', but when you've got two children with special needs, that's very difficult to find. Problems can occur if the AS partner is able to cope with one child but then another comes along, which completely changes the family dynamic. It's that saying of 'two's company and three's a crowd'. Life becomes difficult when you have to try and adjust to be even and balanced in terms of time and attention.

Max '*asked for help as he felt suicidal*'. Yes, depression is common, and I'm surprised there weren't more references to it in other chapters in this book.

Max goes on to say, '*Our daughter has put my wife on the shelf now, and it has broken Trisha's heart.*' She's had her heart broken quite a few times. '*This experience brought out the "crisis husband", and since our daughter's departure I have remained connected to my wife and our son.*' Yes, I'm glad to hear this and that Max has a good rapport with his son. The sadness is that if their daughter has Asperger's and has decided to jettison the family, it could potentially be a lifelong decision. One of the characteristics of Asperger's syndrome is 'black-and-white' thinking. It is very difficult for a person with Asperger's syndrome, once they've made a major decision like that, to change their mind. It is quite likely that there will be no contact, which is hard, especially if she's going to have grandchildren.

Trisha closes by stating, '*I have learned you can't change an Aspie. You can only set the boundaries and not let yourself be consumed by autism and AS.*' Those are words of insight and wisdom. She ends her contribution by writing, '*I am more balanced now in looking after myself*', and states that their relationship is a happy one. It's great that Max ends on a positive too: '*I have come to love and appreciate Trisha more over these last five years together...*'

It's great closure.

Max's natural approach as a parent seems to be practical rather than emotional or nurturing. Is it common for an AS parent not to need that emotional connection with their child? How might this affect their relationship?

Trisha has commented that '*we both have different approaches to raising our children*'. There can be an issue with two different styles of parenting. It's a classic problem not just confined to AS/NT parenting. Mum tends to be understanding and compassionate, giving love and guidance, whereas Dad may be seen as providing criticism, punishment and discipline. Of course, in years gone by when you had very strict families (and in some cultures today) that was acceptable. But in modern, Western society it's not. So being an AS parent in our society can be hard on the children as well as on both parents – the NT parent may feel frustrated, angry and sad that their partner may be missing that emotional link with their child, and the AS parent may feel that they are doing their best and still being criticized.

Max is looking for the day when he can say 'job done' – it's that feeling of needing closure. When you're at work or at home doing the washing-up, you know when a job is done, but, as a parent, it's never done. And that can be hard. There's a lovely phrase, 'You're only as happy as your least happy child.'

Why do many people with AS seem to be able to cope with the demands of work but are not able to cope with the softer demands of home?

Because work is, for the most part, predictable and the Aspie knows what's expected of them. Max describes how he '*immersed [him]self in the safe routine of work*'. The problem is that home can't run like clockwork with clear policies and procedures. School can, work can – but home doesn't. And that's a challenge.

Trisha's comment here is that '*Max would help with all the housework and get up to see our son, but he was not there emotionally for either me or our daughter because it was too overwhelming and confusing for him.*'

But this is not just a case of things being overwhelming and confusing. Max wouldn't know what to do. He can change a nappy, he can do the washing-up. If he can see what to do, he'll do it and the job will get done. Max says, '*I became good at fixing the problem once I was made aware of the problem.*' That's important. Once a problem has been clearly and unemotionally articulated, the AS partner will very likely do all he or she can to help rectify it. Often, the lack of reciprocity or action stems from not understanding what the problem is in the first place.

Emotions or 'softer' demands can't be seen and so are harder for a person with Asperger's syndrome. When it comes to the social or emotional needs of his children and his partner, Max doesn't know what to do. It's overwhelming and confusing and he is frozen in uncertainty and really cannot determine what to do. It follows that, if you fear making mistakes, you minimize the risk of failure by doing the least. The less you do, the less the risk of failure.

Now, Max also talks about his focus with work and his lack of attention and connection at home. An AS characteristic is that when you're engaged in work it's as though you have a different persona. You're in a different universe and the universe of home doesn't exist. You don't have an alarm going off to prompt you to call your wife to say you'll be late. So the conversation may go something like:

AS partner: I was fine at work, why would I need to tell you I was going to be late?

NT partner: But I cooked a meal.

AS partner: Well we can heat it up.

NT partner: I was worried about you.

AS partner: But I was fine.

NT partner: Yes, but I didn't know that.

AS partner: But I was fine. If there was a problem, I would tell you.

This lack of communication can easily be construed as uncaring, but is an inability of the AS partner to see things from another's perspective. It's the Aspie way.

Trisha says that Max and their son 'speak the same language'. Does having AS help a parent to communicate and connect with an AS child or can this double the challenges?
It is interesting that one of the characteristics that can occur in parenting is the AS parent having a favourite child who can do no wrong. The AS parent is totally supportive of that child, the other child or children just get in the way and are often criticized. Once that golden child leaves home, the favouritism may transfer to another child. This can cause huge jealousy from the others when that 'favourite' child can get away with things that the others cannot.

We also find that there tends to be a polarization between an AS parent and an AS child. These personalities will either attract like magnets and get on very well, understanding each other and 'speaking the same language', or oppose each other and be unable to get on at all. You might think 'surely, if you're both AS, you should understand each other'. But this isn't guaranteed.

Now, Trisha goes on to say that Max *communicates with [our son] better than he does with me*. So these (AS) magnets are attracting each other, they're getting on fine, which is great. But it also means that their son can only cope with one parent and it is black and white for both of them. So it's almost as though the son hasn't got two parents, he's got one – his dad. And his dad is everything.

People with Asperger's are described as chameleons, adapting to situations. If people with Asperger's can do this, why don't they do it all the time?
Because it's tiring. They will do it if there's value in it for them. So, when you're negotiating and compromising with an Aspie, you've got to say quite bluntly what's in it for you but, more importantly, what's in it for the Aspie. If there's nothing in it for them, why should he or she make all that effort? So you say, 'If I go, you'll lose your housekeeper.' You have to negotiate from a self-centred point of view, not necessarily the altruistic.

When the AS partner is able to be the life and soul of the party and be very sociable it is hard for the NT partner and the children to understand, and not take personally how this can appear, by choice, to be switched off behind the closed doors of home.

12

Socializing

Socializing

ERIK'S STORY

I lost my hearing at three months old due to meningitis. I was raised orally (speaking rather than signing) and learned to sign when I was 18 years old. I became immersed in the deaf world around 22 years old. I received a cochlear implant when I was 12 years old and it benefits me in hearing environmental sounds. I was also diagnosed with Asperger's syndrome around four years ago. I currently live in Silver Spring, Maryland (after being raised in Massachusetts) with my wife who is deaf, has cerebral palsy and who is a neurotypical (NT). I have one brother who is almost four years older than I am.

I have an Associate's degree in computer science from Springfield Technical Community College, a Bachelor's degree in psychology from the University of Massachusetts, and a Master's in social work from Gallaudet University. I currently work at the Independent Living Skills (ILS) Day Program at Deaf-REACH, an organization that works with people who are deaf and either have mental illness or are intellectually challenged. My role is to help operate the day program by planning and facilitating activities and outings, in addition to keeping up with paperwork for the people on my caseload.

During my childhood years, I encountered several moments where people perceived my behaviours to be 'odd'. For instance, I would stim (self-stimulate, usually through physical movements or sounds) and flap my hands while spending time with relatives and during activities. At that time, it was not clearly understood why I engaged in these behaviours.

During my adult years, I encountered several occasions where it just didn't make sense to me why people behaved the way they did and why social 'rules' were set up the way they were. Even though I put effort into trying to make sense of social behaviours and rules, I sometimes still didn't 'get' it. This would lead me to outbursts and meltdowns – for example, I would pick up a kitchen chair and shake it. Or I would pick up a bag and swirl it around over my head.

I began to understand social behaviours and 'rules' thanks to a friend who was mentoring me, and, through individual therapy, I learned about Asperger's syndrome. It explained why, throughout the years, I had thought and behaved the way I had. People with Asperger's syndrome have more of a challenge 'reading between the lines' and picking up body language. Also, these people tend to become over-stimulated in social settings, which can lead to meltdowns. The scope of my therapy sessions revolves around discussing various situations I have experienced and then discussing, as well as refining, coping strategies. This cognitive-behavioural approach is helpful in my therapy sessions.

One of the very first coping strategies that I learned and am still using now is how to think in certain situations. For example, in the past if I started to become frustrated (or over-stimulated) because I just couldn't 'get' something, I would tend to go up to the wall and bang my head on it. Learning coping strategies helps me to stop this reaction. As I approach the wall, I can tell myself 'this is not healthy'. I have learned a healthier approach, which is to articulate my feelings and simply mention that I am feeling frustrated. I also tell myself that I don't have to 'get' something right at that moment and that I will eventually 'get it' in time. Additionally, I ask people to be patient with me and explain things to me in logical rather than abstract terms.

One of my favourite coping strategies is the use of codes, because this strategy is as structural and logical as it can be. For example, my wife and I have a code ('rainbow') between us. This is used when something that either one of us would like to have or do is truly important to us and not getting it would risk resentment developing. Suppose I want a new iPad very badly, I would tell my wife, 'I would really like to get a new iPad so that I can play some games that I can't download onto my PC. Rainbow.' At work, when there is a crisis with one of the people whom we serve, a staff member would come up to me and use the code 'Red'. Using codes eliminates my need to try to read between the lines and helps me to get right to the point of the message.

Another coping strategy I have is using other people as resources in social settings. My mentor tends to give me cues during social gatherings – this includes facial expressions such as a quick, subtle shake of the head indicating that I should not be doing something, and mouthing of words such as 'talk later' when I start to ask an inappropriate question during a gathering. I also sometimes write down my questions, like 'Should I be asking about her financial situation at this time?' on a piece of paper and pass it on to someone whom I trust at a dinner table. Then, the person would write his/her reply on the paper and pass it back to me. Another strategy I use is asking people what certain topics or jokes mean if I don't 'get' them. When I ask for additional explanations, I sometimes ask if it is the right time to ask when I am unsure. I ask for explanations in certain social customs too, such as what I should do if I meet someone I know on the street while walking to work: 'Would it be polite for me to reduce my walking pace so that I can walk with the person? Or would it be OK if I just continue at my current walking pace? How do I figure this out?' When I ask people these questions, I sometimes end up explaining to the person about Asperger's syndrome so that he/she can understand better why I am asking the questions.

Since I often find social situations to be over-stimulating, unstructured and too fast-paced, I tend to take breaks on my own (and inform my wife and others in advance if necessary). When I take breaks, I tend to go window-shopping, buy myself a cup of coffee and/or sit and relax with whatever I bring in my bag (which my wife calls my 'survival kit'). In my bag, I tend to have a book that I am truly into, my Nintendo DS handheld system, sometimes my iPad, and sometimes my laptop. For example, when I was attending a wedding for a friend of ours, at break time I quietly sneaked out of the reception area, walked over to a tree and sat under the tree facing a pond. I used the time to admire the beauty and read a book. About half an hour later I was ready to go back into the reception area for a while. Later I would take another break. Instead of sitting in one spot, I sometimes walk around a place and explore its surroundings.

I find it very helpful to get as much advance information about an activity or event as I can. For instance, my wife and I went to a funeral service for one of her aunts. Before the funeral, I asked my wife about what I should expect from the service and why things were being run the way they were. My wife explained some aspects like people dressing nicely in order to show respect to the person who died, a white cloth being placed over a coffin representing life after death and the fact that we don't bring food or drinks into the service demonstrating our effort to focus on the person who has died.

Yet another technique that I find useful is to connect with people in a way that I can tune into and understand. I have been performing magic shows since age 12 (and started practising magic at age five). Putting on magic shows is one structured way that I can connect with people. Also, I set up game shows and unique ways of giving gifts during holidays. For instance, I would set up a treasure hunt for a Christmas gift – the first clue would be wrapped, this clue would lead to the second clue, and so on. Another example is to set up game shows like *Jeopardy!* This is a game show we have in America where people have to guess what is being described through clues. The magic shows and game shows are structured ways for me to connect with people.

I believe the most important coping strategy is to accept Asperger's syndrome as part of who I am and to embrace my whole self. I also find that being open about my Asperger's to people is a very useful tactic. Before an important discussion (such as an interview for the day program to be re-certified to provide services for the next fiscal year) I would inform the person or people I am interacting with about my Asperger's syndrome. I feel better when people know about my Asperger's beforehand as it helps to prevent misunderstandings and to facilitate clearer (and more logical) communication. At times, I naturally bring up my Asperger's during discussion. I remember during an interview last year I informally mentioned my Asperger's. I explained that, due to my Asperger's, I used my co-workers as tools to help me pick up body language of the people we serve that I might otherwise overlook. After that, the interview became softer in tone, more concrete and more interactive. I felt freer in asking questions about what the interviewers were asking me (such as whether the staff know the side-effects of medications taken by the people we serve). I also felt able to ask for feedback in how I could improve my work. By the time the hour and a half was up, I didn't want the interview to end!

I strongly believe that taking charge of yourself, in terms of self-awareness and self-growth, is the key to coping with Asperger's syndrome and social situations. I have learned that it is not an overnight process, and my therapist has been reminding me that the coping strategies take practice. If I hit a low in terms of managing a situation at one point, I just tell myself that I will get better with practice. Additionally, the strategies can be changed and/or refined through the course of life using the resources I have available such as my wife, relatives, friends and books. With practice, the coping strategies will become more and more natural, and Asperger's syndrome will be embraced as a part of me as a whole person.

CHARMAINE'S STORY

The backgrounds of my partner and me are social work training as well as being deaf with dual disabilities. I also have cerebral palsy (CP). Being part of deaf culture, the value is on communication as an accessibility issue using American Sign Language (ASL). We value our deafness and deaf culture highly and communicate in ASL. Our mutual friends come from the deaf community. We are interested in many activities but enjoy being homebodies as well.

I grew up in an oral (non-signing) background and attended oral, mainstreamed schools in America. I am the eldest of five children. Our family is very group-oriented. As a result, I too am very much group-oriented and value family and friends highly. I function as a chameleon: mimicking the values and social norms of various communities, such as hearing, deaf/ASL, deaf/oral, deaf/CP, etc.

I went to Gallaudet University, the world's only liberal arts university serving deaf/hard of hearing students and got my Bachelor's in social work in the 1990s. I then attended the University of Pittsburgh, Pennsylvania for a Master's in social work. I found work and moved to Washington DC as a social worker within the child welfare system. By the time I met Erik in 2005, I was quite comfortable with my identity and was independent.

Erik came from a similar background – going to an oral school and being mainstreamed as well. He also had a hearing family. He learned ASL late, in his teens. His family is very individualistic-oriented. He got a Bachelor's in psychology in his home state along with a Master's in social work from Gallaudet. Erik works in a social work agency with clients who are deaf/hard of hearing and affected by mental illness or are intellectually challenged. We first met at a social work workshop but didn't start dating until a year later when Erik moved back to Washington DC for a job with the agency where he is currently employed.

In the early days, there were (and still are) times when our backgrounds, approaches and AS/NT minds clashed. In America,

Valentine's Day is a big thing for couples, and my parents are no exception. They always exchanged roses, cards and lottery tickets. My expectations were hopeful: a flower or a card would be wonderful in acknowledgment of our feelings for each other.

For our first Valentine's Day outing, I asked Erik to meet me at our favourite Vietnamese restaurant and surprised him with a teddy bear, a picture frame and candy. He was a bit cranky and tired – especially after a challenging day at work. He said 'Thank you' and that was it. No warm greeting, no 'Happy Valentine's Day' – and no present.

When I asked him whether he knew what day it was, he said it was Valentine's Day and that he would have a gift for me at a later time. I took that to mean that he had forgotten and that the gift later was an excuse. A fight ensued – with me in tears and him leaving in a huff for his apartment. I called my parents and told them what happened. I explained that they exchanged gifts and cooked a special dinner and that was how I envisioned Valentine's Day for Erik and me. Mom pointed out that each family is different and that maybe Erik's parents weren't big on Valentine's Day. She asked 'How did Erik's parents do Valentine's Day?' and I told her I didn't know, which got me thinking.

A few days later, Erik met up with his best friend and mentor, who told him that everyone has a human need to be acknowledged and made to feel important. She encouraged him to start thinking of surprises for me. Later, Erik surprised me with a paper flower and told me, 'I am sorry for minimizing the importance of Valentine's Day. I learned through a friend that it was important to you. I am sorry that I didn't have anything for you on that day. Here is a flower. It will never die and it will always be fresh.' Hugs and kisses were given that day, as well as forgiveness.

I learned, through that incident, that NT rules about celebrating special days like Valentine's Day may not be recognized by an AS person. I've had to learn not to take offence or feel dejected because of it. And Erik has had to learn to ask what my expectations are for particular occasions: flowers, a card, something simple or extravagant. We've also learned that we need to be aware of our own and each other's love languages: whether we see love as being expressed through talk, gifts, touch, time together or acts of service. That way, we can show love in a way that is important to the other person.

Erik is fiercely practical. Last year, when my mobility scooter overturned on my way home in the dark, I was able to flag help from a driver. That driver assisted me, got the scooter upright and made sure I could get home. When I got home, Erik's first words, upon hearing what had happened, were 'Is the scooter OK?' He followed this up by going over to the scooter and giving it a full check.

I flicked the living room light to get his attention: 'You forgot to ask whether I'm OK', I said. 'Are you OK? Are you hurt? Do you need an emergency room visit?' – I prompted him by asking him to repeat these questions after me. I then asked him for a hug. Later on Erik told me that he felt he didn't need to ask me if I was OK since I was standing in front of him and didn't look hurt. Erik couldn't see beyond the practical (that I was physically OK) to the emotional (that I needed to feel cared about and reassured). The NT rule here is to suspend logic and focus on empathy – checking on the wellbeing of your partner before thinking about the practical aspects and whether money will need to be spent. The AS/NT compromise is for the AS partner to check on the emotional and physical wellbeing of the NT partner first. Later, the expense/repair part of the problem can be considered.

Erik is very much a hands-on person. He likes activities and does not like chat, even in the deaf community. He has quite a few creative strategies to help him cope with social occasions, such as putting on magic shows or game shows like *Wheel of Fortune* or *Jeopardy!*. Using structured activities helps him tune in better with the group.

Erik finds himself challenged daily by work situations, friends' dynamics and family situations – parents, siblings and marriage. I often find myself as a social mentor that he tries to tap into to understand what's happening. For his part, he helps me with driving as well as the housework.

One area in which he has had to adapt is to tell me when he needs time out during social situations. A few years ago, during a family reunion at my aunt and uncle's, Erik disappeared for an hour and a half without letting me know where he was going.

I did know of his plan; he'd told me that he needed a break beforehand – but he didn't tell me that he was taking a break at that particular moment, or where he was going. Mom got worried after not seeing him for a while. I started looking for him in all the usual places: restroom, car... he wasn't there and neither was his backpack (his 'survival kit' that includes his DS game system, book and laptop) so I knew he must have gone somewhere for time out. My mom initiated a family search by sending my brother and uncle to look for him in their cars. After 30 to 45 minutes of searching, I happened to find him sitting behind a tree – reading a book and enjoying his break. He was totally oblivious to the search that was initiated on his behalf.

We've learned from each other in this area: I've learned that he needs time out to recharge and that this isn't him being 'rude', although it might look this way to outsiders. He's learned that he needs to let me know when he's about to disappear, where he's going and how long he will be. Erik also needs to accept that, although break times are essential, so are family times, and that he needs to balance his break times with inclusion in some family activities. Family members need to remember too that this time out is Erik's survival mechanism, which he needs as a result of being wired differently. They shouldn't be hurt or offended as he is the same in all situations, including with his own family.

Since we are both social workers, we have placed a high value on being self-aware over the past nine years. We've taken advantage of individual therapy and do our best to communicate with each other as fully as possible. It's not been an easy journey; it's been painful at times but, in the end, it's been worth all the tears. We've developed codes for us to tune in to each other better, we've had to learn how to communicate and listen to each other, we've learned how to interpret and break the NT rules. Our relationship may be unusual, but it works for the both of us.

Tony Attwood's Commentary and Q&A

Charmaine's description of Valentine's Day illustrates a tragedy in AS/NT relationships that often occurs: when romantic expectations are not realized and the NT person has to cope with fewer pleasures in life than might have been anticipated or expected. In this relationship it seems that Erik learned from a friend what was important to say or do. Mentors are very important for the person with AS. Sometimes that can be within the family, sometimes it's someone professionally or someone in a friendship circle who can give advice independently. Charmaine says she's learned not to take offence or feel dejected. That takes time, and initially there may be confusion, self-blame and anger before the realization that something was not done maliciously.

Charmaine talks about having to guide Erik in social situations. Often, the NT person finds themselves as a social mentor to their partner with Asperger's syndrome. They're forced to take on the mothering role when, really, they're looking for a partner. At times it might feel almost as though they are living with a teenager and having to do a lot of educating in areas that they thought would not be needed. This is bound to affect the relationship. To enjoy intimacy with someone you also have to mother is very difficult. You have to detach yourself and play different roles in different circumstances. In some areas of intellect and insight the AS person is almost at genius level and then, a moment later, they can be behaving like a toddler, which is very confusing.

It's interesting that both Charmaine and Erik are social workers. In Asperger's there is often a very strong sense of social justice, and indeed many people with Asperger's syndrome do have careers in the caring and educational professions. That may work well in the workplace but, of course, home circumstances are very different.

Finally, Charmaine and Erik use codes, and I do recommend this for couples: there may be a phrase, comment or sometimes even a look that says to the AS partner: 'We've already prepared for this. Roll out the script, this is what you're supposed to do.'

How direct do neurotypical partners need to be about what they want from their partners and what should they do if their AS partner keeps on making the same mistakes?

You need to be very direct. In a way you have to fight Aspie with Aspie, which means being blunt. If you camouflage what you say in niceness, it's lost amongst all the words. So it has to be: 'This is what's happening, this is what you do.'

I was talking to a partner with Asperger's syndrome recently and he said that 'in a conversation you don't have a highlighter pen'. I thought that was very perceptive. So what you have to do as an NT partner is to emphasize through your words as though you were highlighting written text. 'This is important – listen to this bit.' Pause. Say it... and then give processing time. Don't rush into the next comment, because the person with Asperger's syndrome needs that processing time – which may be a couple of seconds – to absorb, analyse and process what you have said. Written words are helpful for the Aspie because they can re-read them. You cannot replay conversation. So, with the written word the Aspie has an opportunity to progress at a pace that they can intellectually cope with. As NT people, we tend to talk fast which doesn't allow the Aspie the processing time they need before responding.

In relation to what an NT partner might see as repeated mistakes of the person with Asperger's, we need to look at the learning profile of Asperger's syndrome. Their mindset is to look for differences not similarities. So an NT in any new situation will think, 'What in my past is similar to this that gives me a good starting point for what to do?' The person with Asperger's syndrome is more likely to think, 'No, I don't like this, this is different. I have no idea what to do.' So you will find that, if something was explained at 7pm on Saturday in the sitting-room then at 7pm next Saturday in the sitting room, all will go well. But if you're in someone else's house or at a different time, then it's a different situation. The NT person may have to prompt the AS person in a variety of situations when you would expect them to be able to generalize. Being very situation-specific is a problem all the way through the life of a person with AS. They take things literally, seemingly pedantically so, and they take literal interpretation. And so the NT partner needs to meet pedantry with pedantry. Sometimes you may have to be incredibly pedantic, for example, stating all the scenarios and settings in which a script or prompt is appropriate, which can make things very tedious. It's like programming a computer.

Charmaine talks about Erik prioritizing the practical aspects of her scooter accident over the emotional comfort she really needed. How common is this in AS and can people with AS learn to re-prioritize?

My comment on this is very straightforward: if the person with AS can't see it, it's not there – and so because Charmaine seemed physically OK, Erik couldn't recognize that she needed compassion or a recognition of what she'd been through emotionally. There's a difficulty in reading the cues that are so obvious to an NT.

Many of the characteristics of Asperger's syndrome are great in a work setting – very practical and problem-solving, and teamwork can be appropriately adjusted because of the value the person has within the team. But, in this instance, it is really Erik not understanding that Charmaine's greatest need was comfort and reassurance, not practical assistance – and that can feel heartbreaking at times. In those unscripted situations, the Aspie priority will always be the default position, which is practical. An AS partner may be able to learn to prioritize the emotional aspect of their partner if and when they remember to put the practical aspects to one side for a moment. But this is incredibly hard and won't come naturally to them.

What practical arrangements can AS/NT couples make to ensure that each gets what they need?

If Erik gets 'time out', my question is, is Charmaine getting 'time in'? And that is what you call it in the relationship. 'You have had your time out, you've been there in your study playing computer games, and now I want my time in. And then you actually schedule time in from your partner, when they will spend time with you and the family, as opposed to time out.

What strategies would be useful in social situations?

First, you need to script the AS individual beforehand so that during the event you can provide them with the code or prompt as to what to do. Then you will need to debrief afterwards, and it is important that this includes commendations for the things they got right. This encourages them to keep doing it because, with Asperger's syndrome, whilst there is a pathological fear of making a mistake, there is also enormous delight in getting things right. So they need to know when they got it right! Second, you identify areas of learning. Rather than saying 'you are at fault, it went wrong' or 'that was stupid,' you term this 'areas for learning'...and then you return to the areas that they got right so that their last memory of the conversation is the positives.

Erik benefits from mentoring and counselling. How important is this?
I think it is very important, but it is equally important that the counsellor knows about Asperger's syndrome and speaks Aspergerese, and by that I mean understands the culture. Major problems can emerge with relationship counsellors whose training focuses on 'How do you feel?' For the person with AS, this is one of the hardest questions to answer because they cannot easily convert thoughts and emotions to speech. So the counsellor has got to be someone who understands Aspergerese, otherwise the person with Asperger's syndrome is going to say, 'That was no use, he didn't understand me. I didn't understand him. I'm not going again.' And once you get that Aspie closure and 'black-and-white' thinking, you are not going to change their mind easily. It is very important that there is a sense of understanding the AS point of view and perspective.

How important is compromise in the AS/NT relationship?
A compromise is generally 50:50. With an AS/NT relationship, it's not. It is 70:30, with 70 per cent coming from the NT partner and, if you're lucky, 30 per cent from the Aspie. The NT partner is going to be far more accommodating and flexible and be able to move far closer to the Aspie than the Aspie can move towards them.

Where to Find Support

The majority of links below refer to support based in the UK, where Different Together CIC was founded. However, you will find that each link in turn provides a wealth of further information and recommendations of globally accessible resources and support.

UK

Action for Aspergers

www.actionforaspergers.org

Asperger and Autism Training Consultants

www.asperger-training.com

Autism Oxford

www.autismoxford.org.uk

Different Together CIC

www.different-together.co.uk

Maxine Aston

www.maxineaston.co.uk

National Autistic Society

www.autism.org.uk

Pasda – Supporting families of adults with autism

www.pasda.org.uk

USA
AANE – The Asperger/Autism Network

www.aane.org

Australia
Minds and Hearts

www.mindsandhearts.net

ASPIA

www.aspia.org.au

Canada
Autism Canada Foundation

www.autismcanada.org

Autism Resource Centre

www.autismresourcecentre.com

Books

Aston, M. (2008) *The Asperger Couple's Workbook*. London: Jessica Kingsley Publishers.

Aston, M. (2012) *What Men with Asperger Syndrome Want to Know About Women, Dating and Relationships*. London: Jessica Kingsley Publishers.

Aston, M. (2014) *The Half of Asperger Syndrome (Autism Spectrum Disorder): A Guide to Living in an Intimate Relationship with a Partner who is on the Autism Spectrum*. London: Jessica Kingsley Publishers.

Attwood, T. (2008) *The Complete Guide to Asperger's Syndrome*. London: Jessica Kingsley Publishers.

Attwood, T. and Garnett, M. (2016). *Exploring Depression and Beating the Blues: A CBT Self-help Guide to Understanding and Coping with Depression in Asperger's Syndrome (ASD-Level 1)*. London: Jessica Kingsley Publishers.

Bentley, K. (2007) *Alone Together: Making an Asperger Marriage Work*. London: Jessica Kingsley Publishers.

Finch, D. (2012) *The Journal of Best Practices: A Memoir of Marriage, Asperger Syndrome, and One Man's Quest to Be a Better Husband*. New York: Scribner Book Company.

Hendrickx, S. (2008) *Love, Sex and Long-Term Relationships: What People with Asperger Syndrome Really, Really Want*. London: Jessica Kingsley Publishers.

Mendes, E.A. (2015) *Marriage and Lasting Relationships with Asperger's Syndrome*. London: Jessica Kingsley Publishers.

Robinson, J.E. (2012) *Be Different: My Adventures with Asperger's and My Advice for Fellow Aspergians, Misfits, Families, and Teachers*. New York: Random House Inc.

Simone, R. (2009) *22 Things a Woman Must Know If She Loves a Man with Asperger's Syndrome*. London: Jessica Kingsley Publishers.

Simone, R. (2012) *22 Things a Woman with Asperger's Syndrome Wants Her Partner to Know*. London: Jessica Kingsley Publishers.

Slater- Walker, G. and Slater-Walker, C. (2002) *An Asperger Marriage*. London: Jessica Kingsley Publishers.

Stanford, A. (2014) *Asperger Syndrome (Autism Spectrum Disorder) and Long-Term Relationships.* London: Jessica Kingsley Publishers.

Weston, L. (2011) *Connecting With Your Asperger Partner: Negotiating the Maze of Intimacy.* London: Jessica Kingsley Publishers.

About the Authors

Tony Attwood, PhD is a clinical psychologist from Brisbane, Australia, with over 30 years' experience of working with individuals with autism spectrum conditions. He is also the bestselling author of *The Complete Guide to Asperger's Syndrome* (Jessica Kingsley Publishers).

Lucy Carman helped with the editing of this book and is a freelance writer and editor who has lived with her AS partner for almost two decades – and has learned many lessons along the way! She and her partner have three children together and the trials and triumphs of their lives are recorded in the blog 'Muddling Through - an Asperger's Tale.'

Joanna Pike is the founder of Different Together CIC, a support network for NT adults in relationships with partners affected by Asperger's syndrome.